DETOX YOUR DESK

DETOX YOUR DESK

De-clutter your life and mind

BY THEO THEOBALD AND CARY COOPER

CAPSTONE

This book is dedicated to the terminally
untidy
(that's most of us!)

The authors would like to thank and,
acknowledge the input of loved ones,
friends, acquaintances, business thinkers,
academics and everyone else who knows
us, for their honesty, wit, wisdom and
anecdotes that have made this a pleasure
to compile.

ABOUT THE AUTHORS

Theo Theobald and Cary Cooper must be one of the oddest pairings in publishing. A Californian academic and media-darling and a streetwise Scouser with quick wit, a no-nonsense approach and a business network to die for.

Theo Theobald is a freelance writer and sometime business professional, with a career that includes BBC management and advertising copywriting. He now runs his own company, Shocktactic Limited, writing and lecturing on management, lifestyle and human interaction. He describes himself as tirelessly enthusiastic and endlessly optimistic and admits that this can be 'a bit irritating'.

Cary Cooper, CBE, is Professor of Organizational Psychology and Health at Lancaster University Management School, and Pro Vice Chancellor of Lancaster University. He is President of the British Association of Counselling and Psychotherapy, former President of the British Academy of Management, a Patron of the National Phobic Society and an Ambassador of The Samaritans. He is the author of numerous books and scholarly articles. He was awarded the CBE in the Queen's Birthday Honours List in 2001 for his contribution to organizational health.

CONTENTS

INTRODUCTION

This isn't a self-help book and here's why: self-help is for people with time on their hands, time to stop and consider what their faults are and how wonderful the future will be when they've finished reading the latest 'book of promises'.

Most of us don't have that time, so we've written this book to save you doing all the work that most self-help relies on; it's more like 'we-help'. We've drawn on the experience of business leaders and academics; more important than that, we've spoken to proper workers, the people who do the jobs that keep our organizations running and, based on their issues and experiences, we've constructed a 10-day detox programme, so that you don't have to. All you need to do is follow the actions we've devised on a daily basis and you'll find you will work more efficiently. The inevitable (and desirable) consequence of this is that you will find some time for yourself again, time to do things you want, which we'd guess isn't reading 'self-help'.

The added difficulty with most other programmes is that they're a lot like horoscopes. Some people believe religiously in them; others treat them with scepticism; and then there are those who claim to be disbelievers but sneak a look whenever they get the chance (it's also true that if they find something they don't like very much, they pretend it doesn't apply to them!).

The success of *Detox your Desk* isn't defined by the *level of trust* you put in it; it's a set of factual statements and practical actions that work. There is no clever interpretation or spin, no smoke and mirrors or bottled snake-oil, just common sense.

Most other books will tell you that your unfulfilled potential is limitless, that you can become President, or fly to the moon, if you'd just *believe*. You might be lulled into a state of misery about the huge gulf between where you are now and where any self-respecting citizen of the workplace should rightly aspire to be. But, for most of us, this just isn't true, the gulf doesn't exist; usually our dreams are *just* out of reach: 'if only we had a bit more money, more time, more influence, more love …'

Detox your Desk doesn't made huge promises; it's just a way of getting more out of your working day, increasing your productivity, maximizing your efficiency and allowing you to go home on time.

That's all, but for most of us, that's enough.

What we say is that the things which drag most of us down, sap our energy day after day and stop us reaching our potential are nothing more than minor dissatisfactions, not huge crisis issues.

It's not that we're *actively* unhappy; we're just *passively* pissed off.

The sources of mild modern misery are usually fairly few and most of us share the same ones. You'd have thought we would have found an answer to them by now, but just like the 'common cold', the cure is more elusive than we'd like.

What is it that detoxing your desk could do which you might not have found anywhere else? There are three key elements that drive the success of the programme: firstly, the idea of operating in a tidy, strictly ordered, zero tolerance workspace is part of the answer – detox is also about a philosophy. Our desk or workspace is symbolic of our lives as a whole. The way we choose to operate during the time-consuming and important portion of our lives called 'work' sets the tone for how we are as people, so it's up to us to make the right choices.

Secondly, there's a recognition that while everyone is different, our ability to sort our desks (and lives) out is equal: all we need is the motivation and the tools. If you claim that you're 'not a naturally tidy person', it doesn't matter, because detox isn't about personality, it's about *procedure*.

If you were unfortunate enough to need heart by-pass surgery, you'd hope that the surgeon had good people skills, allied to a bedside manner that was reassuring, but more important to you than their personality is their ability to stick to the procedure. How would we feel if they suddenly decided to get all creative and 'blue-sky thinking' halfway through our op? 'I tell you what nurse, this time, just to see what happens, why don't we try attaching the tube for the left ventricle into the hole for the aorta?' No thanks.

'Procedure' is about doing the same things the same way, every time you do them, *every single time* you do them; something which is not only heartening if you're under the surgeon's knife (no pun intended), but also when it comes to detoxing. So, you needn't feel that the process you're about to undergo will turn you into some kind of tidying-up robot; your personality is still free to exercise itself in whatever eccentric ways you choose. It's just that now you'll be able to do it in a well organized environment, with more time on your hands.

The third important element is that of 'inter-connectivity', the blindingly obvious fact that everything we do has an impact on everything else. You can prove this to yourself by making up your own 'why test', which starts with a general rating of dissatisfaction.

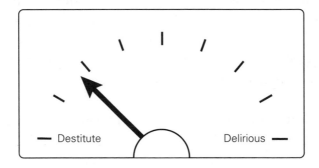

Mentally move the arrow to the position that best sums up your level of satisfaction at work

If you're even mildly dissatisfied, think about why, then connect your answers together. It might look something similar to this:

> *I'm dissatisfied at work.*
>
> *Why?*
>
> *Reason 1:*   *Because I have no energy any more.*
>
> *Why?*
>
> *Reason 2:*   *Because I'm constantly stressed.*
>
> *Why?*
>
> *Reason 3:*   *My stress is driven by guilt.*
>
> *Why?*
>
> *Reason 4:*   *Because I never have enough time for the important things in my life.*
>
> *Why?*
>
> *Reason 5:*   *Because I work long hours.*

Why?

Reason 6: *Because I want to provide for my family.*

Why?

Reason 7: *Because that is my duty.*

The 'why test' works differently for each of us, but starting with any given dissatisfaction, you always end up with a loop, where one element is driven by another, which in turn is connected to one more, showing that unless we break the circle, we'll never be able to unravel the interconnections. That's part of the objective with this method.

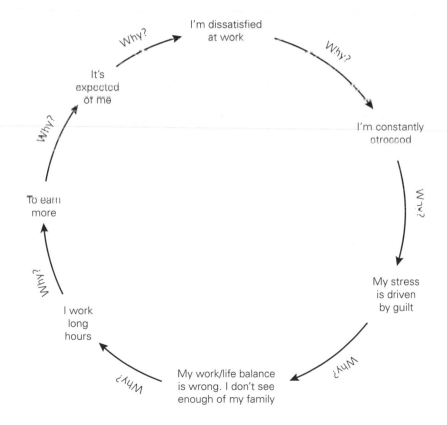

It's worth saying here that the subtitle to this book, 'De-clutter your life and mind' is a critical element too. Having the chance to free up some valuable thinking time is a by-product of what you're about to embark on.

So, our desk detox is *symbolic*, it's *procedure-driven* and it's set in an environment of *inter-connectivity*. These are the three key principles of the programme.

Detoxing your desk, your timekeeping, your finances or anything else isn't about huge changes that, in a matter of weeks, will make you unrecognizable to your friends and family. It's much more to do with small, daily changes over a 10-day period, followed by ongoing 'farming' as a method for sustaining your progress. You only need to detox once (though reminding yourself about it now and again will help), then with regular maintenance, you can keep yourself in that state for ever after.

Ten years ago, detoxing your body was all the rage, though like lots of self-improvement schemes, it was soon replaced by something new. It seemed that, like most programmes, it had a downside. You had to give *everything* up (except the things that no one likes), with the result that most people ended up in an irritable state, with blinding headaches.

This programme isn't nearly so extreme, unless you think that common sense is a bit edgy. None of the changes is difficult or dangerous; all of them can be maintained in the long term, and that combination is the basis of the programme's success.

There is a rule that's compulsory though, because even if the suggestions we make aren't difficult, they're not optional either. This is a 'zero tolerance' programme, so if you want to pick and choose which bits you buy into (like when you're reading the horoscopes), you might as well know right now, the method simply won't work and you'll be worse off than when you started. You'll feel that, yet again, you've attempted to change things and failed.

The promise is that this is a 'once-only' way of changing things; get it right first time and you won't need to keep on returning to the start to try again.

HOW TO USE THIS BOOK

Just picking the book up and reading it would be fine; you'd soon get the hang of where it was going. But to make life easier and give you the chance to get the most out of your detox, here are a few notes of explanation.

There are three sections, the first is **'Analysis'**, and before you feel inclined to skip over it, this provides a really strong set of reasons for detox, all of which will help when you undertake the programme. It's more than just an interesting look back at the way we used to work and how organizations function now; the insight it provides is aimed at helping to increase your motivation levels, to enable you to be the best you can and as efficient as possible.

Having the motivation to detox is all very good, but without the right tools for the job, you'd flounder at the first hurdle, so *Section Two* of the book looks at **'Method'**. Here you'll find all the necessary support for your detox: it'll make you think about how to overcome the obstacles you'll meet, equip you for completing the tasks you'll be set and prepare you for success.

The bit that everyone wants to jump straight into is **'The detox programme'** itself in *Section Three* of the book. It's a 10-day map of actions, thoughts, reflections and behaviour that will change the way you work.

THINGS TO LOOK OUT FOR ...

Scattered liberally throughout the text there are sign-posts, memory joggers and introspective tasks to think about, each of which has its own icon, as follows:

 Pause for thought

You'll find lots of references to raising your level of consciousness, because this is one of the really important elements of change. Having time to stop and think is a great benefit, so when you see this icon, set a bit of time aside to pause and ponder.

 Note to self

Sometimes we all need to set reminders or just log important actions that need to be taken. A diary is the best place, but if you have your own separate system (maybe an electronic itinerary on your phone) then feel free to use that.

Each time you see the pencil icon (above) make the 'note to self' it specifies.

Do it now!

Too often we put off the things which will make our lives easier. The paradox is that the effort we put into these actions usually turns out to be less than the energy we lose by *not* doing what's nagging at us. It saps our energy, so when we say do it now, we mean it!

Real life

During the course of our research, we've come across many stories that support or enhance the theories we've put forward. You'll find these marked in the text by this icon and they give you a chance to reflect on what is happening, or has happened, to other people.

Quotation

The text that follows is supported by the input of interesting business figures from organizations as diverse as IBM and the NHS. Over and above their wisdom, there are quotations from historical figures and heroes of our age, and these are marked out by the 'speech icon' shown above. Hopefully, their wisdom will help to supplement our thoughts; you can memorize any that really appeal to you and quote them at appropriate times!

Pertinent Post-its

Have you ever got to the end of a chapter of a book and wondered what it was about? Not because you couldn't understand the content, but simply because your concentration wavered at the vital moment.

To act as a memory jogger, we've included the most relevant tips and bullet points from each of the chapters of this book on a 'Pertinent Post-it' which summarizes what you've just read. These notes appear on all but the final section, which outlines the detox programme.

DEFINING THE PROBLEM OF TOXINS AND ADDICTIONS

We're not like cavemen any more, fighting for survival against predatory beasts and the harsh elements; instead, because we pretty much have everything we could ever want and need, we've invented our own *virtual* sabre tooth tigers and sub-zero temperatures.

The dangers that face us, like stress, addiction and over-indulgence, are every bit as life-threatening, but, before you can hope to be free of them, you first of all have to admit their presence.

If you like 'the odd glass of wine' or you're carrying 'a few extra pounds' try scaring the hell out of yourself by finding out how bad the problem is. There are lots of websites on health and well being, so it's not hard to find an 'are you drinking too much?' quiz, or an 'optimum weight for your height' chart.

What works against most of us where this is concerned is when we fall into the trap of 'denial by comparison', which means that we think we're okay because we use other people as our benchmark, rather than proven medical fact. So, if you're 'not as fat as x' or you 'drink much less than y', the truth might be that you're still in the danger zone; it may be time to reassess yourself. This 'denial by comparison' is especially dangerous if you use the contestants in reality television shows as a basis for judging your own misdeeds.

The same applies with detoxing your desk. Just thinking that you're 'a bit untidy but it could be worse' (worse, that is, if someone dumped the waste bins from the canteen over your desktop and left a dead rat in the top drawer), is not a realistic starting point. Your state of mind has to be about *admission* of the problem, because it's only then that you'll do something about it.

The reality of the situation is that only a small percentage of our society is dreadfully addicted, most of us are just mildly overindulgent; however it's not the *degree* to which we exercise our excesses, but the *regularity*. Stopping that is at the heart of successful detox. A little too much (alcohol or untidiness), over a long period of time, is the very factor that can leave us with permanent low level dissatisfaction.

So, the first stage of being able to detox is owning up. It's the ability to say to yourself that you don't like the way things are now and you're not going to live with them any longer.

Step two is just as simple: it involves making a deal with yourself. This, again, is where toxins and addictions share common ground. If you've ever found yourself in a situation where you've pledged to give up or cut down on something because you've been nagged into it, you'll know just how much you can come to resent whoever nagged you. It makes sense that our only real chance of success occurs when we're doing it for ourselves. Detox because you want to, not because someone else says you should, and try to remember afterwards, when you're going around being evangelical about the process and what it's done for you, that not everyone may share your enthusiasm. They might still be in denial.

 WHAT'S ON YOUR DESK?

You might like, at this stage, to give yourself a benchmark against other people, not so you can pretend you're much better than the average, but so you get a feel for what needs to be done. In our research we asked people what was on their desks, and some of the responses are listed below. Think about how this compares to your own workspace.

◆   Computer monitor, keyboard and mouse
◆   Files and folders
◆   Stationery (pens, pencils, staplers, paperclips, desk-tidy, scissors, highlighters etc.)
◆   Trade magazines
◆   Research documents
◆   Reports
◆   Invoices
◆   Orders

All of this is the kind of thing you'd expect to find, it's the 'tools of the trade', but the key question to ask is, 'Why is it there?' With very few exceptions, the things that surround us are dormant for most of the time: we mean to get round to reading reports, but never do; our intent with files and folders is that we action them, but the reality is we can only do one thing at a time. The harsh truth is that most things that surround us are only serving to confuse our thinking, to mess up our desks and clutter our minds. Often, we keep things only for reasons of *heritage* or *habit*, i.e. because they've always been there, or we've got into the bad practice of holding on to stuff that's not needed. Everything that's on your desk that isn't being used is a toxin which is distracting you from the job in hand. (Please note that the real definition of multi-tasking is doing more than one thing at a time … badly!)

If you now think that there are some items in the above list that could be binned or put away elsewhere, you've made a good start, but there is worse to come. The next list incorporates some of the totally useless things that people hoard. We haven't made them up, people actually admitted to their presence.

> 'To do two things at once is to do neither.' Publilius Syrus (Latin writer of maxims)

- The last person's work (i.e. the files and folders that belonged to the person who 'used to sit here')
- Postcards (from last year)
- Cuddly toys (donated by loving partners or children)
- Instructions for the photocopier (that was replaced by a newer model four years ago, yes that's right, four years ago)
- Stress toys (now coated with dust)
- A broken hole punch
- Novelty paperweight
- Several blobs of Blu-Tack

There were more, but we've listed enough for you to start to see the picture. Sometimes people hang onto things for some kind of misguided sentimental reasons; what use are the postcards once you've read them, other than to remind you that someone else had a better holiday than you? How likely is it that the photocopier will one day come back and, if it did, would you need the instructions to know how to work it? In all of these cases we returned to the same question, we asked people, 'Why, what are these things doing on your desk; what purpose do they serve?'

Now think about your desk, list all the things on it and ask yourself why they're there; if there's no good reason, it's time to detox.

SETTING YOUR PERSPECTIVE

The differences between us are remarkable: no two matching sets of fingerprints or DNA or, for that matter, no two personalities that are identical. This means that we can both look at the same thing and come up with different interpretations of its form, or its ethos, or its implications. There will be an opportunity to assess your personal attitude to detox a little later, but be aware that outsiders might see the process, with its zero tolerance approach, as restrictive, retentive, even excessive; that, of course, is their prerogative and it's based on their perspective.

Our preferred way of looking at detox is that it is a 'design for life', and here's an explanation why. The concept of design is subjective: what one person thinks looks wonderful, the next might be appalled by. However, something that combines function and form with efficiency and aesthetics (i.e. it looks good and it works well), tends to get most people's vote. Here's an example:

The benefit of good design

Ever since grapes were first trodden and wine first made (which is probably quite a long time ago), man and, increasingly, woman too, has faced the tricky task of uncorking the bottle. If, as a teenager, you ever attended a party of such sophistication that someone had brought a bottle of warm Liebfraumilch, you'll know how frustrating it can be to be deprived of the contents, all for the want of an opener. Probably, three essential items were gathered together, a fork, a tin of Elastoplast and the telephone number of the nearest Accident and Emergency department.

From the fork onwards and upwards through the 'food chain' of openers, comes a curious mixture of implements. There's the Swiss Army Knife corkscrew, which digs into your hand so much you have to drink alcohol to dull the pain; the conventional turn and pull version, great for getting the veins to stand out in your temple as you attempt to release the stubborn cork; there's even a spiky gas-powered thing which looks like it might shatter the bottle into shards if used incorrectly; and then there's this:

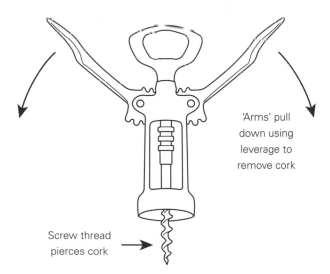

'Arms' pull down using leverage to remove cork

Screw thread pierces cork →

This thing of great beauty builds on the principle that corks are most easily extracted once you've managed to spear them with something curly. Its stroke of genius is the twin handles that are pulled downwards, using the power of levers, rather than brute force, to ease the cork gently from its housing.

The point is that there are many ways of uncorking a bottle of wine, but by far the cleverest and consistently the most efficient is the cantilever corkscrew. It's all about good design.

When it comes to your desk (and elsewhere in your life), this detox is the way. It is to untidiness what the cantilever corkscrew is to a cork; it's been designed to work, it's a design for life. Whether it's a glass of wine or an efficient workspace, you can see that there is always some reward in applying the right design.

So, if a colleague's perspective on your impending new tidiness and methodical nature is that you're 'just being a bit picky', remember that there is only one truly effective and efficient way to run things; it's been designed. Detox involves precision. It's not an opt-in or -out system; it's a set menu.

Your critical colleagues will be forced to acknowledge your success when you prove that this regime makes you better at your job, able to leave on time with everything done and a whole lot less irritable or stressed than they are.

The fact that in future you will operate using a system that says everything has a place, and it should reside there until needed and returned there afterwards, will have some people queuing up to call you a control freak, but this too is only a matter of perspective. There's a world of difference between a control freak and someone who is *in* control.

Finally, to wrap all of this up, another quick word about addictions. If you've shared some illicit pleasure with friends or colleagues in the past, let's say smoking, for example, you will find that they will take it personally if you choose to give up, almost as if you have betrayed them in some way. Some may even try to tempt you back, others will claim 'you'll never manage it', and this is because of something we referred to earlier, 'denial by comparison'. When we're all in it together, when everyone is overindulging in their vice, it really can't be too bad for us to be involved as well. It's a brave person who stands up to this kind of peer pressure, but soon you find that there's another group you can join, like the non-smokers, for example.

If those around you denounce your detox as just another fad, remember it's not them you're doing it for, it's *you*; so let them comfort themselves with 'denial by comparison'. Be your own person.

SECTION ONE

ANALYSIS

ONE

OUR GENERATION AND THE WAY WE LIVE TODAY

The idea of time travel appeals to us all; it opens up possibilities of a fantasy world where we could be whoever we wanted in the past, or live a different existence in the future. Such a fantastic flight of fancy attracted the attention of H.G. Wells when he wrote *The Time Machine*, and persists right through to today with *Doctor Who*.

But fantasy it is. We're stuck with the time when we're born. With luck, we get the average of about 75 years, then it's all handed over to the next generation, with whom we lost any faith a long time ago. That 'three score and ten and a bit extra' time slot sets the context for our lives; it's the backdrop against which we exist and it is highly significant in our pursuit of happiness and fulfilment, because we judge our ability to achieve our ideals within our own generation. Success is a relative term, according to our own era. To get a sense of perspective, we're going to use the next section to compare the present to the past, both in terms of work and life in general.

What would it have been like a couple of generations ago? For most of us, even trying to imagine how our grandparents lived is really hard.

Certainly, there wasn't nearly as much material wealth. Only the privileged few drove cars, work was hard and long (okay some things haven't changed!), poverty was rife, hygiene standards were poor, life expectancy was much shorter and rates of infant mortality were much higher. For men, most of the time was spent working to provide shelter and enough food for the family; women, too, toiled tirelessly, giving birth to and bringing up the next generation, without the assistance of automatic washing machines, effective detergents, fridges, microwaves or a thousand other things we take for granted. Frankly, they must have been knackered most of the time.

So, when it was all such a struggle, literally just to stay alive (side-stepping malnutrition or starvation, avoiding disease, cheating the grim reaper), how much time do you think they spent deciding between whether to install another en-suite or have decking put down in the back garden?

This isn't to criticize our generation's level of aspiration or desire for material wealth; it's just an attempt to show how increased prosperity releases us from the concerns our ancestors had; we seem to have replaced this with our own problems.

The future is a mystery, but we can *look back* and learn some lessons. When life was much harder, there was considerably less time to worry about our modern obsessions, the greatest of which seems to be ourselves. How likely is it that you'd have heard your granddad in the Working Men's Club confessing to his pals, 'I can't quite put my finger on it, but I just don't feel "centred" at the moment', or his wife confiding in a friend that she sometimes found it hard to cope with the burden of guilt around balancing her kids and her career (especially when she quite often, secretly preferred her career)?

Self obsession is the burden of our generation, just as rickets and impetigo (a couple of long-gone ailments) were in theirs. Rather than lament what we've become, we should be more inclined to celebrate the fact that the difficulties we face are much less than those of past generations. Which of them wouldn't have swapped their 'tin bath' for a whirlpool Jacuzzi-action hot tub? Or for that matter, our worries about long working hours versus theirs on the possibility of *no* working hours.

If we have become collectively more egocentric, we shouldn't be ashamed; it's simply about facing up to the norms of the time we're living in, and in exactly the same way that our ancestors 'got on and made the best of it', so should we. Nor should we think that selflessness is a thing of the past, or that mankind as a whole can't be redeemed from itself and act according to the benefit of all its citizens. To do that though, the journey has to start with us. Start small, focus on what's going on here at home, and change ourselves and our lifestyles in a positive and enduring way, right now, for a better version of us than we've been used to in the past, and who knows what impact that might have on people around us? Really, that is what this detox is about.

But does it work? So far everyone who has tried it has reported positive, long-lasting benefits with no apparent negative side effects! The results show an increase in efficiency with the benefit of freeing up more time; when this is used productively, through making conscious choices, levels of satisfaction have risen; we've even had reports of people indulging in 'a long leisurely stroll' or 'a couple of hours with the Sunday papers'.

Every generation has its own set of adversities to cope with. Who knows what'll happen to the next lot, with their huge advances in technology, but with their social problems and conflicts? One fact remains, which is humanity's ability to adapt and survive.

No amount of wishing for a time machine will make it appear. Instead we should just accept the hand that has been dealt to us and make the very best of it. We can't change our time, but we can change ourselves; doing it through detox can mean we have the best of times.

GETTING THE BALANCE RIGHT

Because of the way work was a few generations ago, the vast majority of people regarded it as a necessary evil.

There must have been those who enjoyed their jobs; craftsmen surely got satisfaction from a productive day's work; so too in the professions you'd imagine that carrying out your duties to the best of your ability resulted in you feeling like it had been worth turning up.

The overwhelming sense, though, is that there was a very clear division between what happened in the workplace and what happened at home. The factory hooter, signalling the end of the working day, was a reality for many, and it would seem that the spirit of it (i.e. a sense that work was finished), was a part of all jobs.

The division is not nearly so clear now. By looking at what has changed, we can get a real sense of the challenges that face us today; understanding 'what we're up against' is the first step to finding some modern solutions, which is what detoxing your desk aims to help with.

A BRIEF MODERN HISTORY OF WORK

Around the time of the industrial revolution, when mass production started to signal mass employment, the balance of power in the workplace sat firmly with the entrepreneurs who ran the businesses. There were few binding contracts of employment and workers had little or nothing in the way or rights. Much of the manual labour that was employed came on a casual basis, sometimes daily.

There's an expression on Merseyside that has survived until today, but has its roots in these working practices and goes a long way to summing up the conditions at the time.

If you want to insult someone on Merseyside (and be sure to think carefully about whether or not you do) you'd say 'der's nothin'downf'yer', translated as 'there's nothing down for you'. This implies that someone is a waster, a useless layabout (as we said, choose carefully!). In the days when the Liverpool docks were thriving, workers turned up each morning and went to see the charge-hand, who had a master list of everyone's name and skills; this early 'database' matched tasks to individual men, so the work could be allocated in as efficient a way as possible.

If you turned up one morning to find that there was nothing allocated against your name, the boss would say 'there's nothing down for you' and you'd simply have to go home and not be paid. If this was repeated again and again, you can see how your reputation in the community would soon be one of a good-for-nothing.

In the first swing of power away from the bosses, the trade unions formed to give workers a collective voice to negotiate better pay and conditions for the good of all their members. In many ways, this helped to redress what had been a very unfair system, but, as with many such initiatives, at some point the pendulum swings too far, as this story illustrates.

TRAVELLING SIDEWAYS

In the broadcast industry in the Seventies, the unions were all-powerful and negotiated allowances for every conceivable change in working patterns or conditions for their members. When travelling to outside broadcasts, some engineers sat in the back of vehicles, working at the mixing desk, which faced the direction of travel. In a technological leap forward, one manufacturer developed a new desk, with many advances and one disadvantage: it was too wide to fit across the vehicles, so had to be installed front to back along the side of the vehicle.

It's said that the union successfully negotiated on behalf of their members, as sitting transverse to the direction of travel gave them motion sickness, so they were compensated with a 'travelling sideways allowance'.

As with all these things, the balance eventually swung back the other way, as Britain under Margaret Thatcher became a difficult place for the trade unions to hang on to power.

When recession resulted in redundancy, the bosses were once again in control as the veiled threat of job losses loomed large over the remaining workers. This still remains the case today amongst many members of the generation that lived through those times.

It's hard to find a worker in their forties who hasn't been made redundant, seen it happen to their colleagues or lived in fear of it; and, not surprisingly, this has proven to be a great motivator, even though it's a rather blunt instrument.

In all the changes in the balance of power at work, there has usually been no malice in the actions of one party (the one in the ascendancy); they've simply been looking after their own interests. However, the way that they have started to behave has often been copied by others in their peer groups, resulting in the emergence of a culture. So, if you see your colleagues in another union negotiating a 'travelling sideways' allowance, it's not long before you're thinking about something similar for you and your co-workers; similarly, if 'threat of redundancy' in one sector is helping to suppress pay increases ('you're lucky to have a job, so don't be asking for any more money'), other business owners will create a similar atmosphere at their workplace.

The result in either case is that the working environment, conditions and expectations coalesce into a culture, with common norms across industry sectors and job types.

Now we seem to have reached a stage where no matter how damaged the work/life balance becomes, we accept it; in fact it has become the case in many circles that a lack of home life is some kind of badge of honour. Have you ever witnessed this with colleagues who attempt a kind of perverse one-upmanship by claiming that no matter how long your working day is, they've done more? They started earlier, finished later, received more emails, attended more meetings, covered more miles, drank more coffee and missed more meals than you? These persecuted peacocks are even worse when they meet new people socially, and show off by comparing how terrible their life is to everyone else's. Why do they do that? Martyrdom, perhaps?

SOME KEY FACTS ABOUT WORK AND JOB SECURITY

The truth is that we live in an era where we're all prepared to trash our work/life balance. Many factors can affect this, but the spectre of redundancy is certainly a key motivator for many people. How scared we are of this depends on many factors, and often the relationship between them makes the situation worse.

Age

It's a fact that the older we get, the harder it becomes to find work, especially at the same level. For most of us, if we really were a high-flyer in our current organization, there would be a queue of head-hunters trying to woo us away to a competitor. If that's not happening then it's unlikely to begin when we are carrying the 'black spot' of redundancy around with us.

It's also true that, for most people, their careers progress over time, so the older we get, the higher up the organization we're likely to be and the more we'll be earning; so as the saying goes, 'the bigger they are, the harder they fall'.

Many people find that change gets tougher the older they get, and our fear of it seems to increase accordingly. We just don't seem to bounce back as well as we once did.

Dependency

The times in our lives when we are most independent are also the ones where we're likely to take the biggest risks; after all if it all goes horribly wrong, what's the worst that can happen? However, when we pair up, and perhaps have children, the weight of responsibility becomes much greater. Now there are people who are literally depending upon you to work, but not in any old job: in a job that has brought them all a level of luxury they've become accustomed to (and a level of aspiration that demands you work harder, longer and more lucratively). Opting out of this rat race voluntarily is tough, having it 'done' to you, can be devastating.

Materialism

Linked to this dependency is the collection of worldly goods that surrounds us all today. Our core base level of expectancy is now way beyond 'a roof over our heads', 'food in our bellies', 'tin bath in front of t'fire'. Naturally, the kids don't want to give up their games consoles, just like we, as parents, don't want to have the indignity of sending back the BMW and changing it for a second-hand runabout.

If you or the kids have never had these goodies in your life, then you might envy others who have, but at least there's a sense that you 'don't know what you're missing', so your ignorance is bliss; however, once you've had it all, you don't want to lose a single little bit of it.

Self-worth

Finally, some – not all – of this materialism is linked to our self-worth. No matter what anyone says, were defined not by who we are, but what we own. A further factor that governs our self image is *what* we do for a living. In cases where people have dysfunctional home lives, work provides an escape where they 'can really be someone'. Imagine how scary it is to face the prospect of having all this taken away from you. No wonder long working hours seem so appealing.

So 'security', or the lack of it, is a prime motivator in making us work the way we do, and as with many things in life, a strongly held perception by a big enough majority of people can soon result in reality. For the post-downsizing generation, the memory of the experience is enough to create a kind of redundancy bogeyman who lurks at the door of every business, making sure you don't arrive late or leave early.

A further contributor to a long working hours culture in the UK is a factor we alluded to earlier: our national propensity to martyrdom. Why leave early and go for a walk in the woods with your nearest and dearest, when you can find a million reasons to stay at work and then moan about it afterwards? If you don't think it's a cast iron certainty that your co-workers behave this way, then try looking them in the eye tomorrow morning and asking them in a genuine tone of voice, 'How are you today?' People generally say this kind of thing:

◆   'Oh, mustn't grumble'

◆   'Okay, I suppose'

◆   'Not bad, I guess'

◆   'Fair to middling'

If any of them replies with enthusiastic fervour, 'Actually, I've never been better; it's great to be alive!', have them stuffed and mounted.

The result of the changes that have happened and the underlying insecurity which makes most of us work longer and longer hours isn't the only factor affecting us; the nature of the work we do has altered too. Many manual roles have been replaced by 'knowledge' jobs, and at the heart of this change are advances in technology. It's not just the length of the working day that is significant; it's what we do during it, and the quality of many jobs today seems to be diminishing. No wonder we're stressed.

THE TECHNOLOGY TRAP

The Sixties saw a period of excitement over emerging technologies and we were told that, in the future, in our lifetimes, we would no longer have to work such long hours; many of the mundane jobs we were doing would be helped or replaced by emerging inventions, leaving us the luxury of leisure, ha-bloody-ha!

Even in the Eighties, the prospect of new technologies changing the way we worked seemed appealing. Imagine being a 20-something sales rep and having your car upgraded by the fitting of a compact disc player. The male members of the sales force always seemed to be more prone to gadget-addiction and you could almost get one to explode if you offered him a mobile phone, even if he did need three friends to help him carry it. Now we can't get away from the damn things, and if you're a rep with a tendency to slope off early for a round of golf on a Friday afternoon, you're pretty much stuffed these days: they can track you down anywhere.

The PC, followed by email, and then broadband, are three further significant developments that have robbed us of our freedom. Add in these stupid hand-held devices that every second person on a London tube train seems to be using, and there literally is no escape.

So, we're a product of our working generation, facing different, but no less difficult, challenges than our ancestors. The balance of power between worker and employer may continue to sway to and fro, but it looks like 'insecurity' is here to stay. Fears over our financial future are commonplace and, if working hours weren't extended enough already, technology – billed as the great enabler – has facilitated a 24/7 working culture. Part of this detox is about taming the beast and restoring a sensible balance.

 PERTINENT POST-IT

◆ Learn from the past, but live in your own time
◆ Start small, aim to build big
◆ Commit to detox
◆ The nature of work has changed from 'manual' to 'knowledge'
◆ Many workers feel insecure in their jobs
◆ A long working hours culture now exists
◆ Advances in technology have helped in some areas, but often they increase stress

TWO

THE CONTEXT OF YOUR WORKING LIFE

On the whole, we're pretty accepting of what our jobs are; why wouldn't we be? We literally 'accepted' them in the first place. But who hasn't been surprised, somewhere down the line, to find that the organization we applied to, which looked wonderful from the outside, is in fact rather different on the inside?

Often the public face of an organization isn't matched by its private persona.

To get us to go and work there in the first place, they have to flirt with us, court us and eventually entrap us; it's a lot like human relationships. Businesses tend to present themselves by always showing their most attractive side; take hotels as an example: when they are trying to tempt us into booking, they show a picture of the best room with the finest view, which is all well and good from a 'courtship' point of view. The whole thing starts to unravel, though, when you realize that only very few people ever get to stay in the best room. So, wouldn't it be better, and more honest, if they showed you a picture of the dingiest room with a view overlooking the kitchen bins and assorted overworked staff taking a fag break? It's a great idea, though highly unlikely.

Behind the glossy façade of all organizations is a 'below stairs' element which keeps the wheels in motion and it's often this bit that we see last – only after we've signed the contract, been through the induction programme and sat at our desk for a week or two.

Some of the disappointment can be about physical elements; for example, behind the scenes of the average shiny, well-presented, beautifully stocked store, there are the staff quarters, where people are degraded, spat upon and flogged to get them to work harder. It's not really like that, but there are definitely two parallel worlds operating next to each other, one much less glossy than the other. If you want to see this in action, try and get a tour around a major football stadium. Once you've walked on the pitch and seen the magnificent vista of the stands all around you, imagined them full of cheering fans and drooled in anticipation over the feeling that must give the players, take a walk down the 'tunnel' and see where the 'stars' get changed. Yes, the medical and fitness facilities are brilliant, but the dressing rooms themselves, well they're hardly Champneys. This even happens in the US, where the money involved is measurably greater. Being taken round an American football stadium by a tanned cheerleader who's learned her script off pat, you'll be told 'how some folks spend millions of dollars re-furbishing their executive boxes each year to give them a new look'. In comparison, it's like a smack in the face when you enter the dressing room and see its battleship grey walls and utilitarian styling.

It's not long, though, before we get used to our own 'quarters', and accept that the best will be kept for the customers, the visitors, the clients or whoever, according to the nature of the business you're in. What is more difficult to come to terms with is the second, more damaging source of our disappointment: the people we work with. It's not all of the people, all of the time, but sadly the way of human nature is that there are usually a few disaffected people in every organization, a few rotten apples, trying to drag the rest of us down to their miserable state of decomposition.

Sometimes they become marginalized, by an optimistic and cheery majority who bash on regardless, but, you know only too well that often *their* voice is the most invasive of all, reaching every ear, putting doubt, dismay and despair into every soul. Their behaviour is just one of the toxic elements that permeate your workspace, your working life, in fact. Detoxing involves curbing the influence that they have on you.

Lock them out for a while, ignore the dowdy demeanour of the servants' quarters, and what have you got? What is your job exactly? Think about it for a few minutes and then imagine that you had to describe it to a stranger. If it's not too scary, move on a stage further and consider what the point of it is.

WORKING OUT WHAT YOUR JOB IS

Having defined your job as an entity is one thing, but trying to decide what it's *worth* is another, so a reasonable starting point would be to suggest some way of assessing it against others.

What would be really handy would be a job evaluation system. Fortunately, 'Google' is able to help here, simply type in 'job evaluation system' and in 0.8 of a second you will have in excess of 53 million sites at your disposal. What seems to us to be even more remarkable is that each and every site will have its own unique system for you to follow. So the truth is that even with conventional job evaluation, the most rigorous systems are open to abuse.

Employment law now protects us against bullying bosses and un-fair treatment, at least in theory, but sometimes job evaluation systems are used to get round this. People get over-promoted or downgraded according to the wishes of bad bosses, by using systems which are open to a lot of interpretation on the value of roles.

So is there a viable alternative to job evaluation? Yes, there is and it's simple; it's just common sense. Begin by making a compari-son between what you're supposed to do and what you *actually* do. (The easiest way of achieving this is to get hold of your job description.) What can happen, over time, is that your job de-scription is anything your boss tells you to do according to his/her whim on the day, but the starting point is to look at what you *should* be doing.

YOUR JOB

Think of a typical day and the duties you perform, and add on anything that you do now which doesn't appear on the official job description. The list will probably have doubled in size. As well as the regular things which weren't a part of the original deal, supplement the list with half a dozen other things which you've actioned on a one-off basis over the last six months; things which have in some small way contributed to the success of the business, either through helping customers or colleagues, or by performing some cost saving function. You remember, that day you stayed late to help Accounts with their office move, humping all those boxes down the corridor, or when you got a chair and a glass of water for that old lady who was feeling faint in your store, or organized the delivery of paper recycling boxes to make the office a greener place. There are tons of them, one-offs, and they never appear on any balance sheet.

The conclusion to all this? Conventional job descriptions don't work, don't matter and don't count, they're not representative of what we do. The reality is that your job is composed of some core duties (you're a sales person, an accountant, an admin. assistant etc.) with a whole lot of peripheral activities tacked on, either on a regular or one-off basis. How well you do this, in comparison to your colleagues, determines your VALUE to the organization, and this value is a measure of your CONTRIBUTION.

How effective you are can only really be measured once you've nailed down what it is you do; otherwise you will end up working very hard on something that no one really cares a damn

'I do think a lot of people are disorganized and don't have a clear vision of the purpose of their job, so they get bogged down in procedures and tasks without thinking whether they are useful or add value.' Lynn Rutter (Consultant, Organization Development, Oxfam)

'Success is simple. Do what's right, the right way, at the right time.' Arnold Glascow (Author)

about and, no matter how well you do it, or for how long, it won't make a difference to you or to the company. Making ourselves VALUABLE is all about *doing the right things well.*

All organizations have a grand plan. Sometimes you'll find it buried under a pile of unpaid invoices in Accounts; in other organizations it's pinned to the Chief Exec's wall. Sometimes it's much more secret than that and only a select few ever seem to know what's going on, but one thing's for sure: you wouldn't all be turning up each day if there wasn't some purpose to it.

THE PURPOSE OF YOUR BUSINESS

Whoever it was that invented mission statements should be thoroughly ashamed of themselves; they are the scourge of modern business, confusing the managers and making the staff feel inadequate. They nearly all start with 'In partnership with our customers' and will contain one or more of the following: 'world-beating', 'best', 'most highly recognized', 'excellence' or 'satisfaction'; and will be totally incomprehensible and instantly forgettable.

If you want a mission statement that means something, take a leaf out of Toyota's book. They launched Lexus in the UK with a mission statement that every single one of their employees understood: 'Beat Mercedes'; what more do you need?

Whatever high-handed objective your organization has set (save the world, eradicate poverty, in partnership with our customers, obviously), you need something a bit more tangible to grab hold of, so in the spirit of Toyota, the following exercise is called 'what I do', and you should be able to complete it on a Post-it note rather than in a vast volume. Here's an example:

CASE STUDY –
THE SHOE SHOP

Graham works as a branch manager of a high street shoe shop. The product is mid- to up-market, recognized as a quality brand, and they cater for men, women and children.

Avoiding any of the language used in mission statements, he was asked to write down the purpose of his job in as few words as possible (take note of Toyota).

Graham wrote:
  'To sell as much product as possible, to meet the needs of our customers.'

There's nothing here about profitability because Graham has very limited influence over many of the cost factors. He doesn't set wage levels, is only able to offer a little in discretionary discount (for shoes that might be shop soiled or slightly damaged) and has to follow a strictly laid down regime on other cost elements like heating and lighting.

The significance of what he's written is his understanding that when someone else is controlling the margins, the only truly significant factor he has influence over is the volume of sales, and because this is a reputable retailer, he is aware that sharp sales methods or hard selling isn't a route to long term customer loyalty.

To establish what the job entails he was asked to answer the question '**What do you do all day?**'

Graham's list is like this:

Let myself in and prepare the shop for opening

Catch up with any news on sales initiatives or staff briefings

Make sure all stock is merchandised correctly

Manage staff to the best of my ability and communicate targets, promotions or policy changes

Approach customers and serve them appropriately

Follow procedures on security and banking

Maintain tidiness of the shop

Ensure self and staff are up to date with new lines and product knowledge

If you're like Graham, it's likely that only one – maybe two – things from your list will match closely with your purpose-of-job statement. Hopefully, everything else on the list will be relevant and useful in providing support for your main purpose. If not, you need to seriously question both yourself and your boss on why you're doing it.

The 'what I do' exercise is great preparation for detox, because it focuses attention on 'where am I now?', and this is vital in cases where change is on the agenda. Having established this will mean you'll have something to look back on to judge how far you've travelled.

MAKING YOURSELF VALUABLE

In a large organization, where lots of people are employed at the same level, to do pretty much the same thing, it is often DILI-GENCE which is the defining factor that sets us apart: whether or not we're prepared to work a bit harder and smarter on be half of the company. Don't be fooled into thinking this means working *longer* hours, as that's the very thing we're trying to get away from with the detox programme.

UNIQUE TALENT, on the other hand, is typified by that rare individual who, beyond their standard job description, knows how to fix things or find things, or who knows someone who's related to somebody who could help you sort that problem out, or who is gifted with their hands or compassionate, or a whole load of other things. Someone like George, in fact.

GEORGE – THE SUPERHERO

George is responsible for the smooth running of the stock room at a branch of a leading high street retailer, which sells food, clothing and household goods. He's been doing the same job for 14 years and has seen at least as many store managers come and go during that time.

George knows how to fix things, from a barcode scanner to a deep freeze, something he occasionally does with great dexterity and finesse, but more often by either kicking it or switching it off and on again. He knows where everything is kept, even when it's not in the place it should be. He's aware of every health and safety procedure and compliance issue known to man and he's worked out that how happy the customers are, bears a direct relationship to the security of his job.

An endlessly pragmatic person, George knows when the system has to be bent to fit in with the real world; his most used expression is 'the procedure for this is x, but what we *actually* do is y'.

George knows his place and is happy with it; he is proud of the company he works for, even though he knows its every fault; and, most of all, George is irrepressible in a cheery and endearing way.

Unlike some of his colleagues, George doesn't moan, carp about the company, try to get away with as little as possible, steal or cheat. In short, George is something of a superhero: a HIGH VALUE employee who combines DILIGENCE with UNIQUE TALENT.

One of the fundamental principles of this detox programme is to release some spare time for us so that we will be able to exercise choice over what we do. It's interesting then when we consider George's job, because unlike many office workers, his time is scheduled and he's paid an hourly rate. For that reason the amount of time his company can benefit from his talents is limited by his contract. The important learning in George's story is that his 'value' isn't based on him putting in extra hours, which most of us in office jobs have been lulled into thinking, but in *what he does* with the hours available.

The choices he makes are sometimes called DISCRETIONARY BEHAVIOUR; literally, this means the things we do which we use our discretion or judgment over, so George may choose to help an old lady with her shopping, in the full knowledge that he might have to work harder on other tasks later on, to catch up. Service led organizations love this type of behaviour, often describing it to their employees in terms of cheesy buzz-phrases like 'going the extra mile'. Not all organizations are awash with 'Georges', in fact we'd sometimes appreciate it if the assistant had gone an extra few feet, rather than lean on the till, looking bored.

The truth is that the vast majority of 'service' principles are based on the kind of old fashioned values our parents taught us. Our literacy and numeracy skills may be a bit weak, we may even be new to a role and not have much product knowledge, but with courtesy, politeness, consideration for others and a real desire to help, we can get through most situations.

While we're on the subject of value, let's not forget that the cause of a lot of work-based dissatisfaction is a mismatch of perceived worth: either we think we're more valuable than the company does (and we all know people like that) or other workers at our level, who CONTRIBUTE less, are paid more than us.

Contrast George's worth to his organization through his use of discretionary behaviour with that of Arthur, whose knowledge made him an asset, but only for a while.

ARTHUR'S DEAD

In a large process-driven export office in the late Seventies, the accumulation of knowledge was VALUED more highly than anything else; in fact, promotion was based solely on the criterion of length of service. Arthur, who was in his sixties, had been around as long as anyone could remember and had worked his way up to the level of section leader, managing a team of 12, not particularly effectively, as 'people skills' weren't really his thing. (The company didn't care much about this, because they rewarded longevity, not touchy-feely, emotional intelligence type things; they'd never even heard of them in the Seventies!)

One night, Arthur suffered a heart attack and died, leaving his colleagues saddened and stunned. Fleetingly, his team and his peers wondered what would happen to the company, but after a respectable period of mourning (about two weeks) his chair was filled by someone else and business carried on as normal.

The point is that, although Arthur's experience and knowledge were worth *something* to the organization, they could be replicated or pieced back together by those he'd left behind. Without being overly diligent or possessing much in the way of unique talent, he wasn't much missed.

The footnote to both Arthur's and George's stories is that, no matter how highly valued we are, or what level of contribution we make, there's no one bigger than the company; so, we might be missed a little or a lot, but it's unlikely that the entire organization will collapse like a house of cards because they no longer have the benefit of our talents, which is worth remembering if you storm out in a fit of anger one day, thinking it'll make a jot of difference.

Knowing what your job is and what your company does is the key to building your value. The amount of hours you put in are of secondary importance, so detoxing will increase your effectiveness, allowing you to leave on time, with no detriment to the company. Everybody wins.

'Choose a job you love and you will never have to work a day in your life.' Confucius (Chinese philosopher)

PERTINENT POST-IT

- Conventional contracts and job descriptions don't tell the whole story
- What you do is often governed by precedent and the expectations of your boss
- You can build your VALUE without putting in extra hours; it's what you do when you're there that counts
- Value is often measured by how positively you exercise discretionary behaviour
- No one is bigger than the organization; use this fact to keep your perspective

THREE

HOW WE FILL OUR TIME

Work is elastic. Time isn't. Although this isn't the hardest concept in the world to grasp, when it comes to detox, it's one of the most important. We've known for a very long time that during slack periods, work expands to fill the time available. Mostly, these days, managers are at the opposite end of the spectrum, with too many tasks to complete in too short a time frame, but what both states have in common is that, however much you vary the workload, up or down, you can never alter the time available: it neither stretches nor contracts.

Here's a selection of things people say about their time management:

◆ 'I seem to spend a lot of time looking for things, either that I've filed away, or more likely that I haven't. I've got thousands of emails that I've read but never deleted, yet still when I'm looking for something specific, it never seems to be where I thought it would be.'

'I long to be tidy but it's just not in my nature. My husband says my office looks as if I've been burgled!'

'My boss once nicknamed me the butterfly; it's because I skip from task to task, landing briefly then moving on. Even I recognize that by the end of the day I seem to have started lots of things, but not managed to finish a single one.'

'If curiosity killed the cat then I'm in grave danger of going the same way, I love to know what's going on, even where there's gossip concerned.'

'I do have a tendency to put off the things I don't like, but that's only natural, isn't it? Having said that, it's very energy-sapping, because it feels like it's always nagging away at me, there's always a bit of my attention diverted away from what I'm trying to get on with.'

'You need a bit of social time in work, just to relieve the boredom and the stress, come to that. If I make the odd phone call to a mate, join in on the circulation of funny emails or pop into the coffee room for a chat now and again, I don't feel guilty about it.'

'When I'm really busy and focused I can get loads of stuff done in a very short space of time; that makes me wonder why I spend so long staring into space or just sodding about during the slack times!'

'It's wall to wall meetings in this place, you've no sooner finished one than another starts; often we hold a meeting just to see if we need to get together for a meeting, it's ridiculous.'

A BRIEF LOOK BACK AT 'TIME AND MOTION'

'You will never find time for anything. If you want the time, you must make it.' Charles Buxton (English philanthropist)

Post-war time and motion studies are the foundation stones of what we now call 'productivity'. They were designed to chart how long it took a man to complete a certain task and then project those figures forward to assess the maximum output of any single operation during any given period; they weren't very popular with the workforce. Let's suppose as a hard working Joe you turned up every day intending to do your best. In the past, there had been an average output of 20 units an hour from your operation and someone set you a one-off challenge of increasing this to 22. Working flat out you achieve the target, but rather than this being seen as exceptional, it is instantly re-calibrated as the norm. Pretty soon you realize that you need to hold a bit back, so when you're next asked to work harder, you claim you're putting heart and soul into it, while in reality, you've taken your foot off the gas.

There's a classic old British comedy called 'I'm All Right Jack!' starring Peter Sellers, which shows how the relationship between staff and management develops under these circumstances. The bosses persist in asking for unrealistic levels of productivity, over and above what they know is possible; the workers have an equally entrenched position, well below what they can achieve; each holding something back for the negotiation.

We're all still carrying a bit of that legacy with us, which means that when we hit a slack period, rather than going to see the boss and saying that we've finished what was set for us, we slow everything down to the point where it magically stretches in an elastic way to fill the day until going-home time.

What we seem to be incapable of doing is letting the elastic ping back the other way. Why can't we look at the task list for the day and decide that we'll get it all finished by 4 p.m., then take the last hour of the day to do something meaningful, relevant and fulfilling?

We don't suggest that everyone has complete control over their workload, but often we seem to be happy to relinquish what little we do have and allow someone else to set the agenda, rather than take the level of responsibility that is rightly ours.

Sometimes management is at fault. One public sector worker put it this way:

> 'We have fixed hours, so even if you finished everything in dou-ble-quick time, you couldn't go home; you might as well make it last the day, because there's no incentive to do otherwise.'

Because of the principles of elasticity (work is, time isn't), we can only be really successful in a detox programme, if we can truly define ourselves as a GENUINE WORKER. For instance, do you go to work with the sole intent of ripping off your employer? Are you determined to do as little as possible and get paid as much as you can for it? Are you oblivious to the performance of the organization as a whole, as long as you're okay?

The vast majority of workers aren't like that at all; instead, they are typified by a desire to see the organization succeed (to pre-serve some long term job security), an intent to do the best job possible and be recognized for it (because it's part of building self-esteem) and to be part of a winning team (which attracts peer group recognition and praise). All of these factors might have some personal pay back for the individual, but there's nothing wrong with that, because along the way the organization gets what it wants, too: dedicated, diligent, caring staff; in fact, GENUINE WORKERS.

GENUINE WORKER

Think of someone you know at work who you respect for their professional ability. If you could see into their soul, it would tell you that they were a GENUINE WORKER. If that person stopped what they were doing every day at 4 o'clock and spent the last hour with colleagues, offering help, being a listening ear, talking to customers or thinking up new ideas to improve the company's proposition, would you be bothered that they had some tasks left undone on their desks? In fact, if you owned the company, wouldn't you stop and assess the outline of their job and decide which things they could ditch, or whether it was time to employ a support person so that they could carry on behaving this way?

CONFORMING TO NORMS

Why is it then that, as individuals, we are so unprepared to challenge the norms of the workplace? If you're genuine, if you work hard and do your best to clear what's on your desk each day, why shouldn't you go home at the time it says in your contract?

The simple truth is that for all the bleating that's done about being too busy, a much greater proportion of the blame for this than we ever admit to falls squarely on our shoulders. The damning fact of the matter is that most corporations aren't well organized enough to be explicit about the tasks we need to achieve; they're good at giving us an end game (more profit, better patient care, higher OFSTED scores), but beyond a vague overview of our part in that, they're pretty hopeless at specifying what's required. Instead this is usually done via a combination of need (someone has to open the shop in the morning), historical factors (the person who held this post has always done that) and 'common sense' workers/managers, who direct the 'shop floor' staff.

There are also 'remote' managers, who provide 'strategic direction' to the organization, whatever that means. Their role is a distant one, rarely mixing with the staff, hardly ever with the customers, but this doesn't seem to stop them from thinking that they know what's going on. Then there are the worker/managers who are part of the operational team, the people who do what's needed, that really make the organization function.

If you are one of a number of genuine workers in the company, it's not unreasonable to think that you could start and finish on time. Our detox aspiration is about keeping a genuinely positive attitude, but not doing a 60 hour week (unless that's in your contract); we prefer to think it's not so much 'working to rule' as 'working to time'.

So what stops us from doing that? Here are five factors that are at the heart of the answer:

◆　　Personality

◆　　Insecurity

- ◆ Survival

- ◆ Culture

- ◆ Self-worth

Personality

Our personality traits are mostly governed by our upbringing, and if this included a strong sense of work ethic, then it follows that we'll believe hard graft is a part of life. As digging coal and bashing rivets seem to have fallen largely into decline in the UK, many of us are forced into transferring our inbuilt expectation of hard work into office-based roles. The modern theory goes that we're now reclassified as 'knowledge workers', though if you've been put through to your average call centre in the last 6 months (and who hasn't), you might seriously question whether this is an accurate description.

However, because our podgy, pen-pushing fingers are no longer turned towards physical activity, we display our diligence by staying longer hours instead; the time spent in the office has become a metaphor for how *hard* we're working – what nonsense.

Insecurity

It's quite natural to feel insecure about the future if you've witnessed redundancy programmes in the past. If you've suffered the personal experience of losing your job, the feelings are even more acute, but what probably drives our insecurity even more than this is being judged harshly by the people we work with.

When everyone is turning up at 7:30 in the morning and staying til 8 p.m. how can you possibly walk out of the door with your head held high at teatime? Maybe it's human nature to think the worst of such behaviour; we might all get drawn into bitching about someone by saying they're lazy or uncommitted, but what if they're just genuine? What if they're hardworking and conscientious, but have the strength of character to stand up and admit to a personal life?

The truth is that detox won't work without communication. A key part of the process is to manage the expectation of those around you, not by setting yourself up on a podium and announcing that you've seen the light and the light is 'five thirty', but that you've made a pledge to yourself, your family and now your employer that you'll do the best you can for all of them, yes, all of them.

Survival

Using elasticity to make the work stretch out to fit the day used to be a natural part of survival; after all, if the boss spotted that you weren't very often busy, perhaps your post could be closed. Now though, the game has moved on considerably as there's an expectation that none of us can fit our tasks into a 'normal' working day, so instead we make them stretch out beyond our contracted hours. You must know someone in your organization who is constantly huffing and puffing about how busy they are, and yet you can never really see what their output is. Be careful, though, someone might be applying the same test to you.

Culture

It's fair to suppose that a lot of our behaviour is governed by what happens around us. A popular television show in the Seventies was the Burke Special, hosted by James Burke. It presented science in an understandable way for the masses and in one memorable show, it illustrated our desire to fit in by playing a cruel but hilarious trick on one audience member. The show always opened in the same way, with James Burke descending one of the staircases that ran between the audience seating. On this occasion, as he reached the studio floor, the entire crowd leapt to their feet and started applauding wildly, whooping and hollering in what can only be described as a rather un-British way. All except for one poor man, who had been deliberately excluded from an earlier briefing.

The idea was to see if could they convince the man to join in if everyone else behaved in this extraordinary and counter-cultural way; in the event, it took less than a second. Burke went on to show the incident with the film slowed down and with the camera pointing directly at the 'victim'; you can see shock, bewilderment and perhaps a hint of panic all cross his face, yet still he rises to his feet, glancing left and right for clues, then cheers and claps along with the crowd.

In exactly the same way, we become 'normalized' into organizations in a very short space of time. During interview and induction we're told all sorts of interesting information that pertains to health and safety, pension schemes, location of toilets and the like, but no one explicitly mentions behaviour; we take all our cues from the actions of the people we work with. Within only a few weeks of joining a new company, we could pretty accurately describe 'the way we do things around here'. Perhaps what is more significant is the negative behaviours that we know *not* to indulge in; we pick up very quickly on what is *unacceptable* and make sure that we don't cross the line.

The following story has been around for a while and it's a great illustration of how culture seeps into our being and drives our behaviour.

The monkeys and the banana

This experiment involves putting five monkeys in a long narrow cage. At the far end of the cage you place a banana and, not surprisingly, the monkeys start to run from their end to reach it. When they reach the halfway point, you spray the monkeys with cold water until they return to their own end of the cage. You repeat the process each time they make an attempt on the banana, to the point where they stop trying.

At this stage you remove one of the monkeys and replace it with a new monkey. The new monkey sees the banana and starts running towards it, but his newfound friends pull him back to prevent him from getting the cold water treatment.

Over time you replace the four remaining original monkeys with new ones to the point where you have five monkeys in the cage, none of whom has ever been sprayed with cold water.

If you then ask any of the monkeys why they don't follow their instincts and run to the banana, they just shrug and say, 'I dunno, it's just the way we do things around here!'

Please note that no monkeys were harmed in the retelling of the above story.

Culture is powerful; it can help tell us how to fit in, but by the same token it often dulls our conscious thought and constricts creativity.

Self-worth

It's hard to know where the cross-over point was; the point where we stopped defining ourselves by who we are and replaced it with 'what we do'. In a largely materialistic Western society, our worth as judged by others is often based on the things we can afford. Status is a big house or a 4x4, all of which is governed by the job we do and the associated money we earn.

It's virtually impossible to go to a social function and meet new people, without being asked 'so what is it you do?' If you answer, 'I get up every day and am thankful for the gift of life, I take time to listen to the birds sing, I think about my friends and family, I try to keep my "I love you's" up to date ...' you would probably be locked up as a headcase.

So much of our self-worth is intrinsically built around what we do for a living, but just doing it is only part of the story; doing it really well and being recognized for that is equally relevant.

Our strongly held belief is that most people are genuine workers, but what constitutes that definition for each of us is a critical factor. If we're setting out to do a really good job, what criteria will we use to measure that? Often, it's the hours we put in that form a large part of that benchmarking process. The big question is, do we need to?

To support the view that our long working hours culture is truly ingrained take a look at a couple of quotes from the Health Service.

> 'To be honest, everyone around here works more than their contracted hours; for most of the managers, they're doing a minimum of 55 hours a week, some even more than that, when you take into account the amount of extra work that gets done at home – email and the like. The truth is that you could do an 80-hour week and there'd still be stuff that you hadn't got round to, no one thinks they'll ever catch up.' **Nick Grimshaw (senior HR manager, North West Hospital trust)**

No matter what your thoughts are on the efficiency of the NHS, things still happen pretty much how they should; the organization continues to function. If that's the case, all the things which Nick talks about not being done can't really matter that much or everything would come to a grinding halt. Reducing the working week to a realistic 40 hours would mean more things left undone, but would any of these be critical to patient care? If we're going to de-clutter our minds and reclaim our lives, the starting point is to recognize the real reasons for our long working hours culture. For the real answer to why some people put in such long hours, the last word on this subject goes to the Health Service's National Director for Emergency Access, Sir George Alberti, who is almost frighteningly candid!

> 'I've always been totally committed to working in the NHS and don't think that necessarily I've had any worse a life as a result of working a 60-hour week rather than 36 hours, or whatever the standard is supposed to be.

'I've always actually looked on family as a jolly good reason for spending quite a long time at work, but that is an individual point of view.'

But is it, Sir George, is it?

PERTINENT POST-IT

- Work is elastic – time isn't!
- We sometimes hold back from putting in maximum effort in case we're making a rod for our own back
- Personality, security, survival, culture and self-worth govern the way we use our time at work
- Detoxing aims to free up time for you, not your employer
- In most jobs, no matter how many hours you work, there's still more to do

FOUR

ALL ABOUT YOU!

Having looked at the way work is today and the reasons behind it, it's important for us to find out where we fit in. We're not living in the nineteenth century, so we need to abide by the protocols of our own age; reflecting on the steps we climb helps us think about the journey we're on, but all this only makes sense if we know who we are and why we're different.

How much we're a product of nature or nurture doesn't matter, it's more important to understand the personality we've got. Our values, preferences, feelings and fears can be analysed to death, but even if we can trace their source, it doesn't increase or reduce their validity. If you always feel uncomfortable in a particular situation, it's pointless other people telling you it's illogical and you simply shouldn't. Where does a fear of heights come from? Is it because you fell off a very tall building when you were small? Probably not (I hope not, anyhow), but just because you've never dropped a huge distance and broken your pelvis, it doesn't make the *fear* any less real.

Similarly 'meeting new people' often makes us uneasy or uncomfortable; do you dread walking into a room full of strangers? Where these feelings come from isn't half as relevant as the fact that they exist.

If part of who we are is genetic, then our problems are compounded by the massive human failing of all parents and guardians, which is 'aspiration-driven-criticism'.

All of us seem to want something better for the next generation. It's not that the sentiment behind this isn't very worthy, it's just that for thousands of years and hundreds of generations we've singly failed to exercise any wisdom in judging what 'better' means, and it seems we get further away from it all the time.

In Western society we have taken 'better' to mean more wealth, education, enhanced career prospects, money and material goods, these being the hoards of junk we seem to surround ourselves with in order to keep up with everyone else.

Relate Counsellor John Akers says, 'We grow up with a lot of criticism; it goes towards shaping who we are.'

People often reflect on the difficulties of their upbringing and pledge to 'make things better' for their own children. In itself this appears to be a very creditable course of action, but it's unlikely that our hardships have been life-threatening. Because your parents' first house only had an outside toilet, you have made it your life's work to ensure that you can afford a house with an extra downstairs cloakroom, but at the same time you warn your kids that if they don't work harder and do better at school, they'll never be able to ensure an en-suite for each member of the household in the future (like it matters).

We are a generation that's constantly on the back foot, and if that's not bad enough, we're going to make sure we pass these feelings on to the next one too.

Add these circumstances to a liberal helping of our genes (if you are a believer in the nature of heredity), give them a good shake in the cocktail maker of life and you're left with an individual personality: something we all have in common, but where no two are alike.

The complexity of our personality is also affected by who we're with, what our recent experiences have been and the environment we're operating in. There is nothing more cheering than to see your bullying boss out in the supermarket, being ordered around by his domineering wife like a little lap dog; or teenagers who are vibrant, life-and-soul of the-party types when surrounded by their peers (particularly those of the opposite sex), reverting to monosyllabic grunters when confronted by their parents or relatives.

Most of the time we are trying to be all things to all people; it's an inherent part of wanting to fit into society. Our ability and level of desire to exercise this chameleon-like quality is often governed by our life-learning experiences. Suffering the discomfort of 'being the outsider' can end with us bending over backwards to accommodate other people and, in the context of our working lives, this is often at the root of our dissatisfaction, as we end up feeling put upon. There's no worse smell than the whiff of 'burning martyr'.

Personality is important in determining the approach you take to your detox, because who we are, what makes us tick and where we want to get to are inherent in our level of motivation to change.

You may already have used every assessment tool available and be so self-aware that one more won't add anything to your knowledge bank, but this analysis is different, because it's geared specifically to the detox programme you are about to undertake, and the results are linked into the thinking behind its construction.

'Know yourself and you will win all battles.' Sun Tzu (Chinese military strategist)

It's not the key to life and would never claim to be; instead, it's an approach that delivers a broad brush result, suggesting your overall type and speculating on how you might behave under certain circumstances, with particular regard to detox.

DETOX SELF-ASSESSMENT TOOL

On a piece of paper list the following statements, A to J, and put your score alongside each answer.

Statement A

◆ I keep my desk at work very well organized and tidy, with everything in its place. *Score 1*

◆ Although my desk at work is sometimes a mess, I attempt to tidy it before I go at night. *Score 2*

◆ I never think about what is on my desk at work, I just get on with the job. *Score 3*

Statement B

◆ I try to keep to the same working day routine, arriving at the same time and leaving at the same time. *Score 1*

◆ I tend to come to work at roughly the same time but leave at different times depending on my workload. *Score 2*

◆ I tend to get to work when others come, but am never sure when I am going to leave because I get absorbed in my work. *Score 3*

Statement C

◆ I like to do the same things more or less every weekend. *Score 1*

◆ My weekends have a similar structure but I allow some flexibility. *Score 2*

◆ I do different things just about every weekend. *Score 3*

Statement D

◆ I plan well in advance for any trip I take in terms of rail/air travel, hotels, and keep to a detailed itinerary while there. *Score 1*

◆ When going away on business or a holiday, I tend to plan some aspects of my trip but leave a degree of flexibility. *Score 2*

◆ I usually organize my business or holiday trips at the last minute. *Score 3*

Statement E

◆ I have a fairly rigorous plan for each day at work and try to stick to it.   *Score 1*

◆ I like to plan and structure my work but I am not always successful.   *Score 2*

◆ I rarely plan my work day. I respond to the most urgent task or what turns me on.   *Score 3*

Statement F

◆ I like everything in my home to be in the same place, neat and tidy.   *Score 1*

◆ From time to time, but not often, I like to change furniture around in the house for variety.   *Score 2*

◆ I frequently re-arrange things at home, buying new furniture or adding knick-knacks.   *Score 3*

Statement G

◆ I get very upset when other people at home create a mess in their room or in any other part of the house. *Score 1*

◆ I don't mind if other people at home create a mess in their own room but I would not accept this in any other room.   *Score 2*

◆ I couldn't care less whether other people at home have messy rooms because I tend to be fairly untidy myself.   *Score 3*

Statement H

◆ I can't stand it when my colleagues at work leave coffee cups or newspapers and things on, or near, my desk. *Score 1*

◆ When colleagues leave coffee mugs or other extraneous things on my desk or near by, I tend to dispose of them. *Score 2*

◆ I don't care whether colleagues leave coffee cups or other things lying around the office. *Score 3*

Statement I

◆ My music and movies are stored on digital drive systems only. *Score 1*

◆ Most of my music and movies are stored on CD and DVD. *Score 2*

◆ I have music on cassette and movies on VHS; the digital age has passed me by. *Score 3*

Statement J

◆ I never eat food that's gone past its use-by date. *Score 1*

◆ I rarely eat anything that's gone past its use-by date, but sometimes check by sniffing it. *Score 2*

◆ If it's there, I eat it! *Score 3*

HOW YOU SCORE

Add up the marks from each of the ten statements and see what the total means below.

10–16

You tend to be a rule-follower and natural detoxer. If someone moves a knife into the fork compartment, or gets toast crumbs in the butter, you find it stressful. For the most part, order and method are a part of your everyday life, so if things get on top of you at work, you find it difficult to cope.

Detox will offer you a design for your desk which will not only help keep it tidy, but free up a bit of thinking space too. You will get pleasure out of using the new system because it will add to those you already use to get through the day.

Take a hard look in the mirror now and again to check you're not getting too obsessive.

17–23

You're pretty well balanced, but there's room for improvement (and you already knew that!). Mostly you like to stay on top of things, but get very frustrated when they get out of control. It's unlikely you've ever got into an unmade bed, but you're not a tidiness freak.

Some of your frustrations with the way things are now will be solved by detoxing, and the strategies you employ in future will make you better organized and less prone to slipping into untidiness.

24–30

You have bought the right book! Though you've always been a bit untidy, you see this as part of your personality and a way of asserting your 'creative' side. That said, you sometimes get annoyed when you can't find what you're looking for or if the file you're working on has coffee stains on it.

Your great advantage over the other two groups is that you will get more benefit from detoxing, because you've got more improvement to make.

Understanding your 'detox personality' is important, but what implications does that have for the way you work?

DILIGENCE AND ATTITUDE

Most people at work feel as though they don't have much control over their jobs, but this simply isn't true. Wherever you derive your job description from, the set of tasks that we're supposed to perform has a huge amount of flexibility built into it. For one thing, who will ever know if there are some things you never do? Secondly, as we've seen, the whole concept of the job description is flawed; it's open to so much personal interpretation. Finally, it's really hard to measure how well or how many tasks can be achieved in a certain time, as there will often be many factors to take into account.

What makes one worker complete more than another is usually defined by their *attitude* towards the employer, but these attitudes, no matter how positive or negative, usually come with a set of associated dangers. Have a look at some typical worker types and think about how similar or different you are to them.

PROUD OF MY COMPANY AND DON'T CARE WHO KNOWS IT

These workers are usually very highly valued, and organizations aspire to convert their staff to this way of thinking. It means that people rarely complain about their pay and conditions, get on with work unsupervised and use their initiative to problem solve and complete tasks (George, who we mentioned earlier, is like this). For the most part, they will be prepared to work extra hours without more money and make personal sacrifices for the sake of the company. What could possibly be wrong with that from an organizational point of view?

Although this is the kind of attitude that most employers would like to see, it has its 'downside' too. There is a real difficulty if people accept that they have no balance between their work and non-work time. Unless they are single and have no friends, this will have a knock-on effect in their relationships, might end up with conflict or the loss of any kind of social time, and the stress that this brings might be too much to cope with. The extra problem with this level of commitment is that people often expect the company to reciprocate in its loyalty, and that just doesn't happen any more; so you might be faced with a situation where such an employee gets passed over for promotion or singled out for redundancy, resulting in a backlash like a lover scorned. These workers are the ones who are most likely to become disillusioned and even bitter, which at the extreme edges can lead them to exact petty retribution on the company.

MEANS TO AN END

Ever come across someone who was solely in it for the money, didn't give a damn about the company and was determined to do as little as possible to get by? For this type, it's often not the company he or she dislikes, but the very concept of work itself. They'd prefer to be sunning themselves on a beach in the Caribbean (wouldn't we all?), and see work as life's greatest injustice.

No matter who they worked for, their loyalty would be rock bottom and in their embittered state they see all employers as 'capitalist states' out to exploit the workforce for everything they can get. Their behaviour is typified by clock-watching and skiving at every possible turn; they take as little responsibility as they can and are generally a burden on their team and their peers.

AMBITIOUS AND EAGER

Sometimes this attitude is associated solely with the young, which is not entirely fair as we probably all know someone who maintains their optimism and energy beyond the age of 25. However, those of us who have been around in business a bit longer, can probably recall a time when we had a bit more enthusiasm for the daily grind than we do now.

Exceptions to the rule are those workers who really have found their true vocation and just love every minute of their jobs. Often this happens in creative industries or the caring professions, where reward is about more than how much you're paid.

Companies tend to love this kind of worker. The only risks associated with them are their lack of experience, and the need to temper their natural exuberance with a bit of 'real world' thinking; otherwise they can become gung-ho, which is fine when you're instigating change, but less good when the status quo needs to be maintained. Team them up with an older, wiser mentor and you can have a winning combination; let them spend too long with the hardened cynics and they'll soon have the stuffing knocked out of them.

A FAIR DAY'S WORK FOR A FAIR DAY'S PAY

These traditionalists have been brought up to believe that you should do your best every day, but that working for an organization doesn't necessitate selling your soul to them. They can be a bit annoying to co-workers when they get up and put their coat on at five o'clock, but the reality is that they probably have the best balance of all of us.

With luck, their commitment and enthusiasm will be high during working hours; it's just that, unlike many of their colleagues, they know when to quit and go home. Employers generally favour these characters, but what they find a bit destabilizing is that they're hard to get close to and tend not to form any lasting ties, and that can mean they are inclined to leave and work for someone else if they get a better offer.

All these types show different attitudes towards their employer. Some of this is to do with upbringing, or early working life experience. Some are embittered by things that have happened to them at work (or not happened, like a promotion when they believed it was their due), but some people are just born that way. The result is that our levels of loyalty can differ wildly.

Having some degree of reciprocity with an employer is the only thing that makes the relationship work, and getting the balance of that right is essential if both parties are going to be happy. In the good old days, there were attempts to do this via the contract of employment, where, theoretically at least, the employer offered a fair day's pay and the employee promised to do a fair day's work. What underpinned the success of this for many years was the implicit promise from the organization that they wouldn't jettison great swathes of the workforce every time there was a downturn in business.

Those of us who've ended up on the wrong end of the redundancy package might have become a bit disillusioned, and hardened our attitude to the people we thought were philanthropists, though how we could ever have believed they employed us for the good of their health is beyond belief.

So, we've got two things now: we've got an attitude to work and a way of thinking about our jobs; and we can combine that with what the job itself entails (this is still a bit blurred at the edges, because of the nature of job descriptions) to come up with what we think our job *should* be.

This combination should help you determine not just what you do all day, but how you do it; it's the linking of task with attitude to provide a whole picture of what the company gets when it employs you.

WHAT'S THE DEAL NOW?

The trendy thing in business now is the 'psychological contract', which seems to be more like a set of ethereal wishes on either side, rather than any concrete deal between employer and employee; vague hopes that the other party will treat you with some degree of fairness. The theory goes that if they can't promise us job security any more, then we might feel better if they offered some kind of substitute. Strangely, this usually seems to take the form of extra training, so that we can hone our skills, making us more valuable and attractive to a competitor. We're not sure we understand this, either.

All this talk of attitude is really important in understanding what work is about now, and the nature of the relationship we should try to foster, because it's only when this balance is right that we'll stand any chance of successfully detoxing.

Whatever your attitude, the point of going through the detox process is to get your work and life in order – just think about how it would be if you had the time you needed to learn the piano, spend more time with the kids, go surfing, read more books, become a great cook, travel the world … Need we go on?

Understanding the type of worker you are now and what it is that has shaped your attitudes is an essential part of preparing for change.

Without some introspection, the detox process will be much harder, so stop and think about the kind of person you are and contemplate how easy or difficult you might find it to alter your behaviour.

PERTINENT POST-IT

- Understanding who we are is part of the key to success
- Material wealth is only one measure of achievement; it may not be the best
- Think about your personality type, but be aware that you may sometimes behave contrary to it!
- We often have more flexibility in our jobs than we might think – start to exercise your discretion over what you do all day
- There's nothing wrong with being proud of your company, but keep your loyalty in perspective
- If you hate all work, forget about detoxing and buy a lottery ticket!

FIVE

GUILT AND OTHER PROBLEMS

The analysis of how we got to where we are now is useful in preparing to detox. Having an opportunity to stop and think about the evolution of work and how we, as individuals, fit into our environment takes us part of the way, but what's the result of this thinking? It gives us some opportunities, but at the same time, we're left with a number of problems to deal with, and it's here that the work/life balance really starts to kick in, because work issues affect how we feel overall.

Here are the top 10 work problems that are a common cause of dissatisfaction:

1   A lack of achievement comparative to our aspirations

2   Jealousy of others

3   An inability to get everything done, or even achieve a reasonable balance

4   Being unappreciated for our contribution

5   Constantly having to compromise, way beyond the point where we would like to

6   Guilt, guilt and more guilt (about everything)

7   Feeling inadequate – socially, morally and professionally

8   Ever-changing objectives (especially when we get close to achieving one)

9   Toxic relationships

10   Personal dissatisfaction with who we are

If you feel all of these things, all the time, you're in big trouble; but, for most of us, each issue drifts in and out of our consciousness from time to time, leaving us mildly grumpy with the world at large. In reality, the problems are smaller than they look, because the inter-relationships between them can be distilled down to a very few key areas of our lives.

Here is how some of these things play out.

FEAR OF SUCCESS

You might expect fear of failure to appear on any list of misgivings, but often it is the opposite state of affairs that drives our behaviour. What indicators can we see that might point to a fear of success being prevalent?

Self-sabotage

One of the running themes of this book is that many of our problems and dissatisfactions are self-imposed – yes, we like to be able to blame others, either individuals (the boss) or an entity (the company), but scratch the surface a little, and you'll find that *we* are responsible for not achieving our full potential.

Do you ever get the feeling that just when everything is going well, you push your self-destruct button? In our lives as a whole this is very common: dieters who've succeeded in losing lots of weight celebrate by bingeing; successful business people make inappropriate public comments about their customers; athletes over-train and injure themselves.

Why is it that we start a working day with only enough on our plate to keep us going until lunchtime, yet regularly end up rushing round at six o'clock, trying to get things finished? With so much influence over how we work, why do we fall short so often?

This subconscious set of actions is being played out most of the time. Sometimes outsiders might think we were taking deliberate and calculated decisions about forcing our own failure. For some people, this is connected to their upbringing, because they are raised to believe that success and achievement isn't their right – in fact, they think that they don't deserve it.

In an attempt to be self-effacing, even the most successful individuals will attribute their achievement to luck and good fortune – 'I was in the right place at the right time', 'I've been graced with good people around me' – rather than proclaim that it was a mixture of their natural talent and diligence that got them to where they are today.

Never getting to the bottom of the in-tray or clearing the backlog of email is largely down to us. This is partly because we have decided not to say 'no' to whatever is thrown at us, resulting in more arriving all the time, but it is also to do with our in-built ability to sabotage ourselves.

BEN SAYS ...

'I really hate the feeling of being ill and having a sore throat – you know, the kind where you wince every time you swallow; at night you lie in bed, just praying to drop off to sleep and you pledge that if there's the slightest off chance you'll recover from this some day, you'll forever count your blessings that you'll be able to eat and drink painlessly. As soon as you get better you forget this pledge and carry on as normal.

'Work is like that for me. If I'm really working flat out and stressed up to the eyeballs, I say to myself that if it ever ends I'll be forever grateful and will take steps to work in a way that never allows that state of affairs to happen again; I'll streamline my systems and get everything in order for maximum efficiency.

'The truth is that when things slacken off (which doesn't happen very often), I slacken with them; all the things that I promised myself I'd do to catch up (filing, tidying up, culling lists of lapsed contacts), all the things that would save me stress and hassle during the busy periods, I still never get round to. It's as if I'm doing it (or not doing it, if you see what I mean) on purpose.'

Comedian Ben Elton based a whole section of his set on exactly this principle, he called it 'stuff to do', and it was characterized by all the domestic things you really must get around to, like paying bills and emptying the kitchen bin, but never do because you distract yourself with mindless activities, rather than get stuck in and solve the problem once and for all.

Our ability to stare for hours into the mid distance, play with bits of stationery and office equipment (be warned: staplers and bulldog clips can bite back), model Blu-Tack or doodle is a wonder to behold, and all the while the email inbox is choking itself to death because it is so full.

The psychological explanation of this behaviour is that work defines our value, and that when we get up to date that value starts to dissipate, so we purposely never achieve that state. You might have heard a boss say in the past, 'I don't care what hours people work, just as long as the job gets done', but none of us really believes that. If two of you who did the same job tried really hard to streamline your activities so that you finished by lunchtime every day, how long would it be before this new-age boss worked out that you weren't both needed?

On the other hand, if you believed that you could go home when you'd done everything expected of you and you'd still be paid exactly the same, would you still be working at 8 o'clock at night? Why not up your productivity to the point where you finished at lunchtime and spent the afternoon at the shops or on the golf course?

The point of detoxing isn't so you can skive off whenever possible; it's for the sake of being more efficient and effective, for the benefit of your employer and ultimately yourself. It frees your mind so that you can make choices.

Unwillingness to change

Ask someone to picture what success will look like and they'll most likely be able to portray it in positive terms. 'I'll have the admiration of my peers, will be materially well off, spend my time travelling and be sought after for my expertise.' At the same time, not far away, will be hidden a counter-balancing set of *fears* about what fame and fortune might hold: 'I'll be expected to know all the answers, others will be jealous and will plot against me, I'll be disliked for my success, I'll be a changed person, conceited, arrogant, uncaring.' Change is scary and anyone who says otherwise is a liar.

In most organizations, the people who are boldly embracing change, much to the envy of the rest of us, are the very same people who are *benefiting* from it; it's obvious that change is a good thing if you're the one who has got a promotion, a pay rise or a greater power base and oh, how easy it is to criticize others for not embracing the new way of working if they end up not working at all as a consequence!

Despite all the brave talk in most companies about our need to embrace change, when it comes to us as individuals, we resist it like hell.

Reticence to volunteer

They say that one volunteer is worth ten pressed men, but the cynicism that surrounds working life often stops us from putting our hand up and proclaiming that we're happy to take on extra. At school, the pupil who volunteers extra is often branded a 'creep' or a 'swot', and it's very common for us to learn that 'doing the bare minimum' is the acceptable way.

As social beings we are often desperate to fit in; teenagers, in particular, feel the need to conform, afraid that being different is inevitably a source of ridicule, so the risk of volunteering is not only that you might fail, but that you will fail *publicly*.

The often cut-throat world of sales is another good example of 'conforming behaviour'. It's typified by league tables of performance. There's a common feeling that no one wants to be at the bottom of the table and there are, without doubt, many who will go to any lengths to be at the top (seen as aggressive by their peers, their self-image is one of 'winner'); but at the same time, there are many, in our experience, who prefer the anonymity of mid-table mediocrity, basing their attitude on the theory that if you get noticed once, then your performance is more likely to be monitored and criticized in future, if you fail to deliver.

> 66 99
>
> 'The greatest glory in living lies not in never failing, but in rising every time we fail.' Nelson Mandela (former President of South Africa)

Risk averse attitude

There's more rubbish talked about risks in organizations than maybe any other subject. All that stuff from the top about how they'd like us all to take more risks; that creativity and competitive advantage are but a hair's breadth away: all we need to do is take a chance. This is followed by the assertion that 'everyone is entitled to make a mistake'; we're even encouraged in this course of action: 'It's by making mistakes that we learn.' With all of that kind of language around, you'd feel pretty confident about risk taking, if it were not for the fact that everyone in the company knows that a risk-gone-bad is often followed by swift, irreversible and disproportionate retribution.

No wonder we fear risk.

Outsider syndrome

This is the feeling that everyone in business (and elsewhere, probably) has when they've achieved some high status position: it's the uncomfortable sense that they're about to be found out. We're very often insecure about our abilities and talents, so that no matter which greasy pole we might have shimmied up, we're forever expecting that a slide down is imminent. Status often goes hand in hand with insecurity, and because of that we believe we'll get a tap on the shoulder at any time and someone will tell us that we've been uncovered as a fake, our number's up.

The closer to the top of a modern organization you are, the lonelier it becomes, which makes it difficult to find anyone to confide in; there's an expectation that you'll have all the answers, so to admit you don't is seen as a sign of weakness. You're unlikely to confess all to your boss, who might form a negative view when it comes to future promotion, your staff will see you as inept and your peers might use your insecurity to gain an edge over you. Things are usually no better when you go home, as your dependents rely on you to deliver, and the last thing they want to hear is that you've over-stretched yourself.

A consequence of this problem is that many workers feel the need to hype themselves up. Nevertheless, we know we're doing it, so when the payoff arrives and we achieve high status, we suddenly start feeling insecure because we may have exaggerated our abilities in order to get here.

INDIVIDUALITY VERSUS CONFORMITY

From our very early social interactions and onwards through the rest of our lives, we face a constant struggle of balancing between being seen as unique, and a desire not to be perceived as 'different'. From the first schoolyard encounters, children with any slight difference can be singled out and bullied (kids are notoriously cruel when it comes to such things). Only a generation ago, a child who had the 'misfortune' to wear spectacles was labelled 'four-eyes'; that phase has probably now passed, as glasses have become a fashion statement, but it has no doubt been replaced by something far crueller and more divisive.

We carry these hard won lessons forward with us through our teenage years, and it is usually only in adulthood that some are brave enough, or sufficiently self-confident, to risk being seen as an individual.

In organizational terms this translates to culture-conformity, so we very quickly pick up on 'how things are done around here' and find ways of adapting ourselves to it. As with risk-taking (see earlier) this is part of a strategy for safety and survival, which is all well and good, but it does have the uncomfortable spin-off of leaving us unfulfilled, if we aren't using our true personalities to their full potential.

'No one can possibly achieve any real and lasting success or "get rich" in business by being a conformist.' J.P. Getty (American industrialist)

MATERIALISM VERSUS SPIRITUALITY

An incredible amount of pressure exists in our society to prove our worth through what *we're* worth and the surest way of showing this is in our consumption. Are cars still the ultimate status symbol for men and clothes for women? Or is it the other way around now? It doesn't really matter because whatever measure you use, you can guarantee that someone will be ahead of you on the motorway or the catwalk.

We might all admire the icons of our age who are selfless, who seem to care little about appearance or worldly goods, but it seems that there are few of us who can emulate them.

Great dissatisfaction can build in our working lives, if we feel that we're not being sufficiently rewarded, and often this is based on no more evidence than the fact that other people *seem* to have more than us.

There isn't really any quick fix for this – no, not even detoxing your desk will cure everything! The only advice we can offer, based on observations of many similar cases, is that each of us needs to embrace the 'concept of enough'. Faced with the most magnificent buffet table you've ever seen, at what point would you stop eating? When would your natural self-limiting mechanism kick in? It's hard to judge as a one off, but if the buffet were to be available every day, you would surely learn when enough was enough.

In exactly the same vein, we need to think about what is enough in other areas of our lives. What number represents 'enough' rooms in our house, 'enough' brake horse power under the bonnet of the car? When do you reach the point of having 'enough' gadgets, or 'enough' clothes (shoes are the exception, obviously – you can never have enough shoes)?

If you keep this at the front of your mind while you're shopping or when some wily retailer has tempted you to 'impulse purchase', you will find that your ability to curb expenditure is increased.

For those shopaholics amongst us, this must seem like a pretty miserable concept. What happens next? Will we ask you to start cutting up your store cards and putting on a hair shirt for work each day? Not a bit of it, because we recognize that 'retail therapy' is fine as long as we also realize that the pleasure-of-purchase is directly related to its rarity value. Under normal conditions, the joy of acquisition diminishes with every material addition in the same category, so the first new gadget you buy really thrills you, but each subsequent one has less of an effect. If this sounds scarily similar to drug addiction, that's because it is: the more you get, the more you want; it takes an ever increasing quantity to get the same hit. So stop, think, and if you do decide to go ahead and spend, at least it will be a conscious choice and you might get some real pleasure from your purchase. (As we already mentioned, none of this applies to shoes.)

MARTYRDOM VERSUS SELFISHNESS

If ever there was an unsolvable conundrum, it seems that this is it, until you realize that both of these states exist only in our heads. If you're truly selfless, you really, genuinely don't mind if you are sometimes put upon by others; it's only if you let it happen grudgingly that you become a martyr.

Similarly, if you have enough self-esteem to believe that you sometimes have to be good to yourself, then selfishness is not a fair accusation – unless, that is, you have an ego obsession which always puts you first, to the detriment of those around you.

What is true is that both states of mind exist in the workplace. You could probably name a colleague who fits into each category at your organization; if you can, do you imagine either of them is happy with their career as it currently stands?

This is not as bleak as it sounds: yes, we face difficulties that cause us dissatisfaction; but most, if not all, of this is of our own creation. Having self-belief, realistic objectives and a balance between raw ambition and some compassion for your colleagues will go much of the way to resolving the issues.

Detoxing your desk is designed to help you do this; if nothing else it should free up enough 'mind space' for you to rationalize your motivations.

PERTINENT POST-IT

- ◆ Most of the things that hold us back are inside our heads
- ◆ Often we stop ourselves from fulfilling our true potential
- ◆ Behaviour can be governed by the culture of the organization we work for
- ◆ Remember that enough is enough; it's your decision
- ◆ Detoxing your desk can free up the time needed to tackle our demons and stop us being self-limiting

SIX

THE IMPORTANCE OF DE-CLUTTERING YOUR MIND

Scientists, philosophers and psychiatrists have tried and tried to figure out how the brain works and, to their credit, they've discovered a lot, but there still remain many mysteries to be uncovered about the way our minds function.

We're not claiming here that we've done what they couldn't and unearthed some new secrets about human intelligence, but using common sense and the application of some logic, we're expounding the following theory, not as fact, but speculation; it's simply a case of 'what if ...?'

Let's start by saying that the number of different thoughts we're capable of is infinite (don't ask us to explain infinity, just run with it for now); even if these thought-choices know no bounds, what if the overall capacity of the brain, although incredibly vast, is nonetheless finite?

THE HUMAN BRAIN, WHAT IF...?

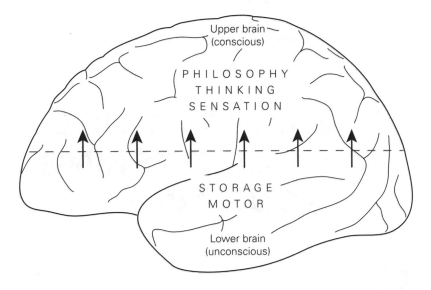

In this diagram, the brain is divided into two parts, shown here of equal size; in reality they need not be so. The bottom half of the brain deals with what we would consider to be the unconscious functions, i.e. those that we quite literally don't have to think about under normal circumstances. There is a further subdivision into 'motor' and 'storage'; the former is to do with all the physical functions our body performs without the necessity for conscious thought; everything from our heart beating and lungs breathing, through to the movement of our limbs. Clearly, the brain is still being used for these things: if you drink a cup of tea, your hand grips the cup and your arm moves it precisely to your mouth, but you don't have to stop and think about it.

We've called the second category of 'lower brain', 'storage'; essentially we've defined it as our memory. In here are huge filing cabinets full of pictures, sounds, smells, sensations and recollections; it forms the knowledge base of our being, it tells us who we are and retrieval of it allows us to tell the world the same story.

The system is good, but not perfect; none of us can recall every-thing we want to, but maybe the concept of 'forgetting' is more to do with not being able to access the right file when we need it (sometimes we remember things again later, when the 'file retrieval' has righted itself), or maybe the brain detoxes itself from time to time and has a good clearout of the less frequently used files. Whatever the case may be, we can probably agree that some finite storage capacity exists. (Conventional, less specula-tive, theory indicates that the more we use this part of our brains the better they get and also suggests that this 'use it, or lose it' function holds true in later life; some feel that those who play a musical instrument or complete a daily crossword may be more capable of staving off the onset of diseases like Alzheimer's.)

The upper half of the brain (according to our diagram) is much more interesting because it houses the 'conscious' bits of our thinking, here sit 'sensation', 'thinking' and 'philosophy'.

Taking 'sensation' first, this is the part of our being that most of us have the greatest struggle with, because often it doesn't operate in the logical way that other parts of our brain do. This category covers feelings like lust, hate, desire, affection, remorse, etc. In many ways, it is these responses that govern who we are and how we see the world.

'Thinking' is the bit of the brain we're all most familiar with because it is highly conscious and is determined by our logic; it's the bit we use to work out a tricky mental arithmetic problem or to decipher a map and understand the route we should take.

Beyond this is 'philosophy', which is a higher level of thinking and might include theoretical concepts and intangibles, the things we can't readily explain or that have no fixed outcomes or parameters, like the meaning of life, the existence of God and all that good stuff.

We have defined four different types of thinker, based on this 'what if ...?' scenario.

1   Cerebral

2   Emotional

3   Ordered

4   Reactive

Cerebral

Cerebral thinkers tend to use the logical parts of their brains in their approach to life. They are great problem-solvers and have the analytical ability to see issues from every angle and then draw conclusions based on fact and logic. Often, they are ill at ease with emotional situations (which tend not to be logical), and instead they seek out cerebral thinkers like themselves.

Emotional

Emotional people are often unfairly categorized metaphorically as scatter-brained. This is because they put their trust in instinct and feelings, following a path that is more governed by 'fate' than logic. 'Sensation' is at the heart of their being, which, on good days, can make them brilliant 'connectors with other people'. If they have a failing, it is an apparent moodiness. This is governed by the pendulum swings of life, which we are all subject to.

Ordered

Ordered thinkers are well-balanced, combining many of the strengths of the above two types; their 'internal filing system' is efficient and they are experts at working out the best way to approach a task. This leaves them with sufficient 'discretionary' time to devote to interpersonal contact, though they can be less 'feelings'-driven than their emotional counterparts.

Reactive

Reactive thinkers let the world happen around them. They are normally too logical to believe wholeheartedly in fate, but they are often unconcerned about what's around the corner, because they operate on the basis that they'll 'cross that bridge when they come to it'. Often they achieve less than their full potential, because they're always waiting for something to happen, rather than instigating change for themselves.

No matter what you're usual thinking style is, what if you were called upon to remember more than you could normally cope with? What if the lower half of the brain then expanded, in order to store all the new information, squeezing the upper part and reducing its effectiveness? We would have less time for higher

Like many models, it's impossible to accurately categorize the entire population like this; but most of us have a leaning towards one type or another. Which 'thinking style' is closest to your own? Are there certain situations when you might break free and act more like another type? If so, what are they?

thinking, our logic might become flawed, but worst of all, the room left for sensation, the part of our lives that most of us prize most highly, might become less effective.

Often we see the result of this in colleagues whose storage has become cluttered and overblown with the amount of work-based data they're trying to remember. One research respondent typified this as 'trying to juggle too many things'. Sensation can then malfunction, causing them to be irritable and short-tempered. Logic can be impaired, too, and solving problems that were once easy becomes a real effort. Finally, the time they have left for 'philosophy' gets reduced, preventing them from being able to see the 'big picture'.

COMMON PROBLEMS WITH CLUTTERED MINDS

We've probably all suffered at some time or another with a cluttered mind; the frequency and length of time this happens for can vary, according to the job we do, the level of responsibility we carry and the out-of-work aspects of our lives that take up space, too.

A great deal of emotional stress, in a relationship for example, can 'use up' brain capacity, leaving us little to play with when we get to work. Equally, office based difficulties can have us pondering our problems when we return home, with the reverse effect happening, squeezing the amount of attention we pay to our loved ones.

Here are some common issues that people face when their brains are over-burdened:

Stress

Adding more and more tasks and responsibilities to our workload often results in stress as our minds struggle to cope. Sometimes short term stress (like a deadline to hit) can be beneficial, giving us the chance to focus on one thing alone, but if the weight of work is continually growing, most of us find it hard to cope and may become unwell as a result.

Lack of foresight

Leaders in business are often called upon to be 'visionary'. They are relied upon to see what's coming next in the market, the economy or their particular industry. Many of us play a part in this process, connecting with the world outside our own business and making predictions about what might change. Sometimes though, because our minds are cluttered, we fail to see what's coming, and both the business and we as individuals can suffer as a consequence. If the organization is performing badly, it might become the subject of a takeover and redundancy might follow; alternatively, the introduction of a new technology could have an impact on how our competitors perform, and it might give them the edge. None of us want our minds so cluttered that we end up saying, 'I didn't see that one coming!'

Forgetting

It's astounding that our memories, which function tolerably well most of the time, can let us down at a critical moment. Have you ever 'forgotten' the name of someone you know very well, or what is normally a very familiar telephone number? The chances are, it's still stored in one of your brain's 'filing cabinets', but our inability to access these things when we want is often the product of 'clutter'. It's like someone has emptied the contents of all our mental files all over the floor and we don't know where to start to find the item we want.

Knee-jerk reactions

Reacting to situations without thinking is often a follow-on from stress, but when we're up against the clock and seemingly have a thousand things to do, we sometimes make snap judgements, simply because we haven't got the time or mental capacity to think things through in the way we normally would. If de-cluttering our minds allowed us the space to think clearly, we would soon get back to being proactive again.

Poor decisions

The process of making decisions is often based on the data we've collected and a weighting of the factors involved, including some thought about the implications of the choices that we may eventually decide on. These are often fine judgements. With clutter in our minds, we often don't think things through, or place too much weight on one factor against another, with the inevitable fall-out of having to live with the bad decision afterwards.

All in all, the difficulties of living with lots of clutter in our minds has a detrimental effect on the way we work and the way we are; even simple tasks become complicated.

We waste lots of time in our working lives trying to remember where we put such and such a file, or stressing over some daunting task; detoxing your desk gives you the opportunity to free up some storage capacity in your brain, which in turn allows you to de-clutter your mind. Achieving that state leaves your upper brain unimpaired to function in the most effective way it can. So although we began by making it clear that this theory is still only conjecture, *what if* you had the chance to use your mind much more often, for the things you find useful, desirable and, literally, sensational?

It's worth a thought.

PERTINENT POST-IT

◆ The human mind works in conscious and unconscious ways
◆ Each of us has a preferred thinking style – what's yours?
◆ Cluttering our minds with stored trivia might reduce our logic and creativity
◆ Detox allows you to de-clutter, so you can think clearly

SECTION TWO

METHOD

SEVEN

FOUR STAGES OF PREPARATION

Analysis is an important part of understanding the principles of detoxing your desk, but there's a time to call a halt and get on with it. To do that, we need to know how detox works, so this next section is all about the *method* of the programme.

This isn't ten top tips, or even three steps to heaven; instead, it is a staged process that will lead you from being a toxin-soaked underachiever to a cleansed and efficient version of yourself who has time on their hands and their demons under control.

The object of the exercise is to eliminate the 'low level dissatisfactions' that plague us every day and return the valuable spare time we seem to have lost, so that we can make some choices over what we do.

Over the coming pages, you'll get the chance to look at your own barriers to greater success and focus your thinking in a controlled way, so that you are fully prepared to begin the detox that follows.

The four parts to detox, taken in order, are as follows:

1   Wake up!

2   Realize

3   Decide

4   Go!

We couldn't get it any shorter than that, except perhaps by leaving out the exclamation marks and they're included for added emphasis. Our thinking is very much based on the Toyota mission statement principle of keeping things simple, and once you've read the explanation of each stage, it should be really easy to remember the pathway you're following.

1   WAKE UP!

Everything has to start somewhere, and with detox it's with the realization that there are some things in your life that aren't quite right, things that need fixing. Think back to the comparison with addictions and you'll see how this process of recognition is the first stage to being able to solve the problem. But it's harder to do than most people think and this is for a very good reason: we live our lives unconsciously.

If you've driven a car for many years, you no longer think about depressing the clutch, engaging the correct gear, setting the engine revs to the right speed or releasing the handbrake at the right time. Take a look around next time you're out and you'll probably see lots of people who've even forgotten how to use a mirror or that cars now come with indicators. We're often so unconscious of the process that we can get to the end of a familiar journey unable to recollect anything specific about it at all – it's that feeling of 'I can remember leaving and now I've arrived, but I don't recall anything in the middle'.

That's how most of our lives have become and here are some reasons for it:

Routine

It's a great thing, routine, because it sets the boundaries for our lives, and it stops us having to reinvent every single thing we do. In fact, it's such a good thing, it's actually at the core of successful detox; it's just that the routine you're about to put in place (of always staying on top of your work) is designed to free you up from the mindless drudge that drags you down (which is part of the routine you're trying to escape from).

'Creativity is to think more efficiently.' Pierre Reverdy (French poet)

The downside of routine, if we're not careful, is that it stifles creativity; it stops us questioning why we do things. Knowing *how* to break with routine is as important as knowing *when* and *how often*.

Pressure and stress

One of the greatest causes of modern stress is the 'stuff left un-done'; the things that we really intend to get round to, if only we can ever find the time. This might be as simple as filing things away at work, or it may be more significant, like taking the family for a day out, or getting in touch with friends who have been exiled to 'Christmas-cards-only' status. If you've got a household to run, it's even worse as the fixing things, decorating and improving pile up on top of the weekly chores of shopping, washing and ironing, and stuffing of mushrooms for that dinner party on Saturday.

We deliberately set our minds to 'unconscious' so that we can cope with this pressure. If we stopped and stressed over the list of undone things, our coping mechanisms would be permanently stretched to capacity. By dulling ourselves down, we actually con-tribute to our own survival. Sometimes, no matter how much we try to keep a lid on things, we have times when we blow a fuse, and when we've calmed down afterwards and look back on the 'explosion', it's usually very hard to fathom why we lost our temper, because the things that stressed us are there all the time. The only thing that seems to change is our perspective and our ability to cope with them.

Expectation

We've highlighted already one insoluble dilemma of modern life, which is deciding on the degree to which we conform and the amount of individuality we express. The latter often loses out to the former, because being different is just too much like hard work; there's the constant need to explain or justify why we've chosen to be different. This means that we feel duty bound to join in with the pack mentality of the 'headless chickens' around us, who are running about trying to make sense of it all (and probably wishing they were brave enough to express a bit of individuality).

If you stopped and thought about this for a second, you'd see how mad it was, but the culture we live within, with its rules and protocols, places demands on our behaviour that we must meet if we're to avoid looking like outsiders. We're unconscious because everyone around us is; sheep mentality keeps us in line, but unaware.

Comfort

We're not always very good at owning up to the problems that face us in life; a prime example is the theory put forward about men's attitude to visiting the doctor. There's no logic to suffering in silence if you think there might be something seriously wrong with you, and yet many men seem to prefer that to confronting the truth. As far as we're aware, *denial* has so far proved to be one of the least effective treatments for cancer.

There are other problems too, like relationships, money worries, job insecurity and self-esteem, which, it seems, we're really good at hiding from. One of our main weapons in this war is our lack of consciousness; when we're dumbed down, nothing seems quite as bad.

With all these factors, it feels like we've just ended up this way, not through any conscious choice but by chance. The pressures of our lives conspire to make us hide away, but in a sense, we have made a choice. By *not* selecting a different alternative, by *not* choosing to do things another way, we end up living with the default option (in this case 'unconsciousness'), and that's the choice of apathy.

Now you can see why we say that the first stage of the detox process is *'Wake up!'*; hopefully you'll also realize the importance of the exclamation mark in emphasizing the need for real action.

The *Wake up!* process is fantastically energizing as it catapults you at light speed from unconsciousness to awareness; it's like a revelation. What is just as exciting is that the journey into wakefulness also makes you realize that there is something you can and will do about the time stealers and the energy sappers.

The key to a successful *Wake up!* is the understanding that there is a different way; this is the stage at which to start thinking about those differences.

Imagine you're four years old once more; very quickly you'll rediscover the key to wisdom that we took just four years to learn and then spent a lifetime forgetting. That key is the word 'why'.

Four-year-olds still live their lives along the rules of the fairytale *The Emperor's New Clothes.* They point out the ludicrous and they ask the tough questions; what's even better is they ask in a big loud voice and they refuse to be 'shushed' – good on them. At the supermarket checkout they ask, 'Mummy, why is that lady soooo fat?', and though you wish with all your heart that it was because she's pregnant, it's probably linked more closely to her trolley full of pies.

Wake up! is all about looking at the world through four-year-old eyes and, for the brave amongst us, articulating the process by way of a loud exclamation.

◆　'Excuse me, why do we have this meeting every week when no one gets anything out of it?'

◆　'How come everyone stays until 8 o'clock when our contracts say we can go at 5?'

◆　'What, actually, is the point of a Blackberry?'

If your workplace isn't ready for loud articulation yet, don't worry, it won't stop you going through *Wake up!* It may just mean you have to do it a bit more quietly.

2   REALIZE

Like lots of words, 'realize' can have different connotations according to its context. It can be a description of a revelation: 'I realized I'd been conned'; it might be a process we go through in order to achieve something: 'At long last, he realized his dream'. Its meaning here is 'to make real', so our interpretation is that the *process of making something real*, is 'realizing'.

Wake up! is the jump start we need to recognize that something is wrong; *'Realize'* is all about defining what that is.

Sometimes we all seem to suffer from a level of tiredness that goes beyond too many late nights; it's the kind of weariness that seeps into our bones and makes it hard to stay awake in afternoon meetings. It is, in fact, not so much tiredness as 'fatigue'. Often it's not because we've just completed the business equivalent of a triathlon, but instead it's down to the constant drip drip of targets to achieve, things left undone, clients who are dissatisfied, colleagues we've short-changed, family who can't remember what we look like, etc. None of these things are hard to fix if we just throw a bit more time and effort at it; the problem is we're spread too thinly.

So it's not that we don't have the ability, or that we don't care or want things to be better, it's just that the *cumulative*, rather than the *individual*, weight of all this is squashing us down. That's where low level dissatisfaction comes from. It's not failing in a

'Be true to your work, your word and your friend.' Henry David Thoreau (American author and philosopher)

wholesale fashion as a worker, or a parent or a friend, its coming up *just* short on all fronts that really gets to us.

The ***Realize*** process defines what our own personal version of the problem looks like. Complete these two stages over the space of a day.

SELF-AWARENESS

First, write down the answers to the ten ***Realize*** starter questions below, which are designed to prompt your thinking about hopes and dreams, as well as looking at what prevents you from achieving them.

This part of the process is called 'factualization'; it's a way of establishing some of the important home truths of your life.

Try to answer the questions as honestly and impulsively as possible, then put the paper away and don't refer to it again for 24 hours.

◆   What are the three most important things in your life? List them in order of priority.

◆   What causes you the most dissatisfaction at work on an ongoing basis?

◆ When was the last time you had an argument (where you ended up shouting), who was it with and why were you arguing?

◆ In percentage terms, how much more money would you need to earn to be 'comfortable'?

◆ Why and when did you last cry?

◆ Who is your worst enemy at work and why?

◆ Describe in 20 words or less what you do all day (at work).

◆ Are you in love? If so, with what or whom?

◆ When did you last have a 'perfect day' at work? What happened to make it so?

◆ Out of all your relationships, which one would you like to devote more time to?

The key to this exercise is to answer honestly and quickly to get the most accurate picture of your feelings and emotions. The reason for putting the paper away for a day is that our perspective alters over time (it's the experience of 'sleeping on a problem' to find it looks different in the cold light of day) and, having just poured out your emotions, it may be that you'll be feeling less logical than normal and the next stage requires logic. It's fine to mull over what you've written, in fact thinking about it can be beneficial in the 'factualization' stage, but don't be tempted to shortcut the process and start trying to 'solve' your issues right away.

Set time aside tomorrow to review what you've impulsively said about your life; before you will be a picture which includes a number of conflicts.

The second stage of questioning is called 'contextualization' where you make some value judgements about the way you live.

◆   What's the ratio of emotional investment that you put into work, in comparison with your outside life? (Express this in percentage terms, e.g. 80:20 or 40:60 etc.)

◆   What is your personal relationship between money and happiness? Would more make you happier, would less make you miserable? Challenge your initial answer rigorously. Ask why money always seems so important.

◆   What value do you put on your time, do you sometimes squander it and, if so, when and why? Think of an actual example.

◆   In your work life make an estimate in percentage terms of how much you feel in control; now do the same for your personal life. Do you think this sometimes varies? If so, what factors cause variation?

◆   Do you sometimes fail to meet your own expectations? If so, what makes you fail and how much influence do you have over those factors?

During the course of our exploratory research we've used this 'factualization and contextualization' process with some surprising results. Many people felt some dissatisfaction with work, but placed most of the blame for this on themselves. Generally speaking, levels of control were high, but rarely exercised to good effect, so the respondents felt that if they 'got their act together' they could complete the tasks that were asked of them more efficiently and in a shorter time frame.

Although money is commonly seen as a driving factor behind why we work and especially the hours we put in, few people thought that a lot more of it would increase their happiness, though some said that less would make life harder. Although on the surface being 'richer' emerged as a desire, there was little substantial data to back up a rationale for wanting such a state. Many felt the 'need' to earn more was forced upon them by a spouse, partner, children or peers.

A number of interviewees expressed the opinion that more money was like a consolation prize. Their lives had become so nigglingly imperfect that retail therapy had achieved the status of 'compensation' for fractured relationships, damaged friendships, stress, poor health, etc.

Nearly all respondents felt that they were letting down the people close to them by working too many hours and that their most enjoyable time was spent with close family and friends. Many also had feelings of guilt over not keeping in touch with old friends or making the effort to visit them.

This set of responses isn't a template for how you should feel, but it gives you something to balance your own answers and emotions against.

The output of this exercise can be expressed by a series of statements. We asked respondents to articulate their feelings and we've summarized the significant themes here:

◆   'I tend to blame other people for my working hours, but mostly it's my own fault.'

◆   'Usually I get pulled in many different directions, but never feel as though I satisfy anyone properly.'

◆ 'It's a long time since I felt free of guilt.'

◆ 'Work is really important to me; it just takes up too much time.'

◆ 'I never seem to know when to switch off; sometimes I'll sneakily check my emails when the rest of the family have gone to bed.'

◆ 'Often I feel out of my depth in work; I'm afraid that other people think it too.'

◆ 'I'm a completely different person at work than at home.'

◆ 'Everyone realizes the futility of what we do, but no one is prepared to break rank and stop it.'

◆ 'I waste far too much time.'

◆ 'I go to work to get away from my family, but I could never tell them that.'

◆ 'No matter how many times I get promoted, I always feel that other people are better off than me.'

◆ 'Other people see me as successful, but I often feel like a failure.'

Once more, we want to emphasise that this isn't included to tell you how to feel, but only to reassure you that other people face similar issues and problems around work as you perhaps do; some, no doubt, are much worse off.

The final part of the *Realize* process is to give yourself a score, as a starting point to the detox process. Otherwise, how will you ever know if it has helped you, except in a rather non-specific way?

 # BENCHMARKING

In each of the following broad areas, mark yourself out of 10; the higher the score, the better you think you're doing.

Control

Do you feel as if you've got a grip on the most significant elements, both at work and at home? This isn't about getting your own way and directing other people; it's to do with how happy you feel over the level of control you're allowed to exercise. For example, if you live with a partner who always organizes your holidays and you just turn up on the day but you're happy with that, then mark yourself highly accordingly (it's not *how much* control you have; it's *how comfortable* you are with it).

Mark out of 10:

Balance

Frequently we think of balance as the amount of time and effort we divide between work and home. Here though, try to

---

see it in a broader light to literally include how well-balanced you feel. Is there sometimes undue stress on you? Are your coping mechanisms often stretched, or do you generally feel okay about the way things are, both at work and beyond? How good are you at juggling the emotional demands on you from other people? Do you think you 'share yourself around' fairly?

Mark out of 10:

Relationships

There's give and take in all relationships, whether work-based or with family and friends. Leaving aside the odd dysfunctional or toxic relationship (everyone's allowed one of those), mark yourself on the success of your interactions, as seen from your point of view. Some friends are 'takers' and no matter how much you give they will never be satisfied. Don't let their attitude influence you too much; instead try to judge objectively.

Because we can't quantify all our relationship in the same way (some are much closer than others), you have an opportunity to mark yourself twice. The 'primary' score is for relationships, spouse, partner, children, family, and the 'secondary' category includes friends and acquaintances.

Mark out of 10 (primary):

Mark out of 10 (secondary):

Happiness

There's a cycle of happiness that runs through our lives. It can operate on a daily basis, according to our successes or failures, or we can judge it over a longer period of time, sometimes even years. We may think of one chunk of our lives to be an overall happy or sad period. Often people will say that their childhood or school days were particularly happy and it's safe to assume that not every day was, but in looking back there is a general feeling of well being. Is that how you feel about your life now?

Mark out of 10:

So, generally speaking, how content are you, based on the marks you've given in each section?

These four factors are important not only as part of the detox process but also in life. They're some of the key building blocks of our existence, so if our starting point is that detox can help make things better, you need to know your overall score. Just add up the total of your marks across these areas; this will give you a personal rating for your potential. How you feel now is an indicator or what you believe you're capable of. Going forward, if low level dissatisfaction is dragging you down, you might not see any light at the end of the tunnel; however, if by thinking about all of this and putting yourself through the detox process, you can get your score to go up, then not only will your potential increase, but your belief in achieving it will too: you will create your own self-fulfilling prophecy.

3   DECIDE

We know that, because of the inter-connectivity of different elements in our lives, changing one area could have a dramatic effect on others. The *Realize* exercise will have given you some time to highlight the insights into your current behaviour. With luck you will have found plenty of things you like, which are generally in balance and only occasionally slip out. Unless you're perfect, you will also have stumbled across things which cause you unhappiness or disquiet; nothing stronger than that, but nonetheless a nagging irritation, which stops you reaching your full potential.

This *'Decide'* stage is included to help you raise your level of consciousness about the past, present and, most importantly, the future. In deciding to detox your desk, the process of change will begin and, although it's designed as a 10-day kick-start programme, the philosophy that it's built on is for life. We know that one-off diets don't work; we need to change our *relationship* with food to create any lasting effect. Similarly with detox – it needs to become part of who we are.

It's desperately important that you embrace the ethos of detox before you start, because not only will there be critics on the sidelines who will want you to fail (like the smokers who don't want you to quit), but to be successful you will need to 'think detox' for a long time to come; until that is, it becomes second nature.

MAKING CHOICES

Decide is also an opportunity for you to think about what occurs when you've finished this book and completed the detox programme. Your *Realize* analysis questions can help you come to a conclusion over what you want to tackle further down the line, and in what order. Maybe you want to detox your finances, punctuality or family relationships; now is the time to define, in your own mind, the priorities for your future.

Most of us have launched headlong into a set of behaviours we thought would make us a 'better person'. The problem with trying to change on all fronts at once is that if one aspect starts to falter, the whole programme can soon hit meltdown. There are two key messages: the first is to tackle one thing at a time – take bite-size chunks rather than the full meal; secondly, *Decide* is about choice; by choosing to spend more time with the family, you can't then use that time to work in. By doing one thing, we're opting *not* to do another.

4 GO!

At last: the easy part! This is where you stop analysing, thinking and speculating over the future and just get on with it.

'*Go!*' is the vitally important activation of everything you've been building towards and its most critical attribute is its most obvious one: *Go!* marks the beginning of your detox.

Without it, a number of things can happen to de-rail you:

Over-thinking

It might be that you'll keep on going round the analysis loop, always wanting to get it that bit more fine-tuned than it is now. This is because most of us have a tendency to put things off, especially when we're facing something we're either unsure about, or already know we dislike.

Not paying utility bills until the red one arrives is a symptom of this, as is remaining in bed until the snooze button on the alarm is worn out; in exactly the same way, we can suddenly become horribly risk averse and decide that it might be safer to indulge in a bit more thinking and analysis before getting started. *Go!* forces you to set a starting point, bringing your deliberations to an abrupt end, no matter how far you've got.

State of mind

We can easily rationalize our actions, but *feelings* are harder to come to terms with. It's important on the brink of your detox to stop and consider if the time is right.

We've already warned against procrastination, but there's a difference between making up excuses not to start and having a genuine reason. Try to choose a time when work is at its least busy (year end is always chaotic, so avoid detoxing then), it's also helpful to think about your private life; if you're just about to go on holiday, save the detox until afterwards.

Once you've made up your mind, commit to the full 10 days, tell yourself it's worth it, then make a start.

Obstacle-finding

Company policy, social norms, peer group behaviour and organizational culture are just some of the obstacles that can stop you detoxing. Without much effort you could list some of your own, but don't bother, because this is the very thing that will prevent you from getting stuck in. Be prepared for the fact that some people won't like what you're doing, others will just see you as plain odd, and you may even begin to question your own motivations at times. Accept that all change is like this and steel yourself for navigating around obstacles or, when push comes to shove, battering through them.

Drifting-in

There's nothing gradual about the start of detox; it's a bit of a shock to the system. Smokers often say that they're giving up by cutting down bit by bit, and this would mirror our definition of 'drifting in'. If you've ever attempted to quit something, (caffeine, chocolate, etc.) you'll know how hard it is and how unlikely you are to succeed by gradually reducing your intake. This is like the modern day equivalent of a death by a thousand cuts; it guarantees a heightened state of awareness over what you're doing and makes sure that you sustain the maximum level of gruelling self-consciousness, which ultimately leads you to crave your passion more than ever. Detoxing your desk has a definite start; it starts with *Go!*

'If we wait for the moment when everything, absolutely everything is ready, we shall never begin.' Ivan Turgenev (Russian novelist and playwright)

In-tox-ication

All the things that are keeping you from reaching your potential, the stuff that saps your time and energy, can block the attempts you make to cure it. 'Yes,' you'll say, 'I'll get round to being organized, when I can find the time,' at which point you're trapped in an endless loop because it is the process of 'organization' that frees up your time. If you stay steeped in your toxins, they will continue to poison you slowly each day. With *Go!* you will define a specific point in time where this is going to stop.

That's it then; that's the four-stage method of detox.

1   Wake up!

2   Realize

3   Decide

4   Go!

You start by shaking yourself out of your complacency and own up to the fact that, although your life is far from being a disaster, it's not quite how you'd like it, either. With a bit of careful thinking and analysis you define the issues personal to you. Using this information, you make decisions about what to do next, how to prioritize the future and the 'critical path' you're going to follow and finally, without further deliberation or re-checking, it's time to start.

PERTINENT POST-IT

- Often we live 'unconsciously'; you have to break this to start your detox
- There are common dissatisfactions that we all share; you are not alone!
- Prioritizing what's important to you personally will give you the energy to change
- When you have all the facts you can make better decisions on what to do with your time
- Actions speak louder than words, so avoid procrastination

EIGHT

TOOLS AND TIPS FOR DETOXING

A staged process, like the one we've described (*Wake up!/ Realize/Decide/Go!*), goes a long way to providing a map for our detox, but if it's going to be successful, we need to pack some essential equipment for the journey; these are the tools and techniques of detox.

PREPARATION

The mistake that many of us make is that we see the end of the day like a finishing line; we're just trying to get over it and then we can go home. This means that we are missing a big opportunity to set up the next day's work, so that we can maximize our efficiency when we arrive the next morning.

How would it feel if you arrived at work and, instead of being in a bewildered state over what the day would entail, you already knew what was on your itinerary? Using that early morning high energy time for 'doing' rather than 'planning' would give you the opportunity to achieve so much more.

DESK MAPS

'Desk-mapping' is a one off process, designed to maximize the efficiency of your physical workspace. It's built on the principle that the more frequently something is needed, the closer to hand it is, and during the process of organizing your equipment this way, you are bound to come across 'desk-junk' (the rubbish that clogs up the drawers or your work surface and never actually gets used at all); this either needs to find a more suitable home or be consigned to the bin.

FUEL

You can't keep travelling when the tank is on empty, so how you fuel your working day is as much a part of your planning as your desk maps and other tools. Your efficiency is bound to drop if you skip lunch, and snacking at your desk makes you look more like a slob than a leader of men (and women).

We're bombarded with advice on diet these days, so we're not going to suggest a prescriptive regime that'll radically alter your lifestyle, instead, simply exercise some moderation and common sense.

Here are some basic fuel rules:

◆　　Don't, under any circumstances, skip breakfast

◆　　Eat plenty of fresh fruit

◆　　Have a light lunch

◆ Drink lots of tap water

◆ Reduce caffeine intake

◆ Avoid high fat and sugar snacks (chocolate, crisps, etc.)

If you're a coffee addict, only part of your craving is for the caffeine; the rest is just a habit. Reduce your intake by having only one fully caffeinated cup per day, replacing the others with decaf. If you make it strong enough, it's almost impossible to tell the difference between the two.

For every cup of coffee or tea you drink, match the intake with a half pint of tap water; this not only hydrates you, increasing your ability to concentrate, but it leaves you feeling less hungry.

Daylight and fresh air are also part of the fuel package and office-based workers who are deprived of both (especially in the winter months) suffer as a consequence. Have you ever gone through a day's training, in a room with no windows? It's virtually impossible to keep up any sensible level of concentration.

Make a point of getting outside each lunchtime, come rain or shine. If you can, go for a walk – it's a great way of de-stressing – but if not, the daylight on your skin and fresh air in your lungs will help to re-charge your batteries for the afternoon.

ENERGY

Although energy is closely related to our fuel intake, it's also the case that we have a natural daily cycle which might be different for each of us. The principle of effectively using your time relies on an understanding of how your personal energy levels vary over the course of a working day; the illustration here shows a common curve of energy over time.

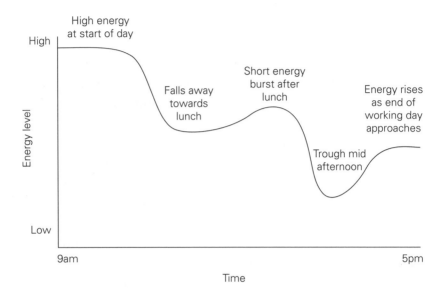

Understanding the shape of your own energy curve is one of the tools you can utilize in the course of your detox.

Whatever its shape, simple common sense suggests that we are more efficient early in the morning than late in the afternoon. The analogy of travelling a journey on foot works well to illustrate this. It's clear that we will cover more ground when we're fresh, in the morning, rather than when our muscles are aching and our blisters starting to smart, late on in the day.

There's an old adage about sleep which says an hour before midnight is worth two after, and as a rule of thumb, this is a good way of viewing the working day, but replacing midnight with noon and sleep with efficiency. So every morning hour of work is likely to be twice as effective as each one in the afternoon, for most people.

Tasks that require active attention or creative thinking should be reserved for our high energy hours. Routine, mundane or repetitive jobs should then be consigned to our lower output time, maximizing not only the number of things we get through but also the effectiveness of what we achieve.

DAY MAPS

Day mapping is an essential part of the detox process; it tells you where you're going!

Intent vs. action!

'We work in an open plan office and every morning my boss comes in and announces in a loud voice "things to do today". He then sets about writing a list, but only ever gets half way through the process, before becoming distracted and I doubt if he ever gets close to completing the tasks on it.'
Joe (Architect)

A day map is a planned journey, so think of it in terms of moving from point A, where you are now, to point Z, where you want to be, with some milestones along the way which will tell you if you're on the right track. With a real, physical journey on foot, you'd soon realize how far you could travel in a single day. It's the same with your office 'day map': there's a realistic limit to what you can achieve. With experience, you learn what an average day's travel would be.

Part of our dissatisfaction at work is driven by our failure to achieve what we set out to do, and we highlight the situation if we devise a task list every day which *never* gets completed. Working effectively involves a process where we can feel good about what we've achieved, so with realistic targets, there's a chance of going home satisfied by what you've done.

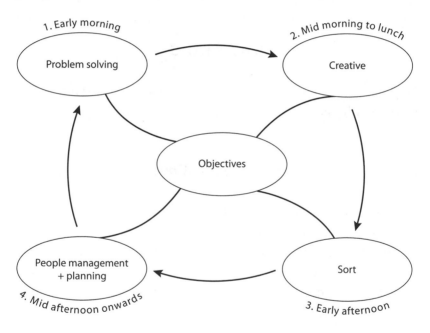

'Day maps' provide an at-a-glance picture of what needs to be achieved, but they rely heavily on self-knowledge of your energy curve. In the diagram above you'll see that objectives are at the centre of the day map, and the 'satellites' represent four major chunks of time. This is so that we can get a snapshot of the type of things we'll do and when.

Decide for yourself where each block of activity is best placed, according to your own energy levels. In the diagram, the early morning slot is reserved for problem solving, as this is when we've said our attention level is at its highest. The second part of the morning is also fairly high energy, which means we've been able to allocate 'creative thinking' there.

From lunchtime onwards until mid afternoon, many of us hit a bit of an energy slump, so rather than battle through some difficult project management problem, we've allocated 'low-consciousness' activity here; it's called 'sort' in the diagram, and includes any admin or other task which doesn't require lots of thinking.

The fourth and final chunk of our day, we've reserved for 'people management', so most of the significant human interaction will take place then.

Once you've constructed your own day map, it needs to be tested over time to see if it works. Soon you'll get a feel for the pattern of your day, and being able to see it in large chunks like this will be helpful in keeping you focussed on the task that you're dealing with. Instead of getting tempted into low-conscious tidying up activities during the mid-morning, you will already know that time is set aside for that, after lunch.

Try a few different permutations of the day map, until you find what works best for you on most days, then use this as a foundation for producing your daily itinerary.

ITINERARY

There are many problems with conventional 'to do' lists, but, not least is the fact that they have no proper end point, so you never know when you've 'arrived'. Producing an 'itinerary' is more than drawing up some vague kind of wish list.

The starting point is to note down all the tasks you have to complete. This is the kind of thing you might expect to see:

Itinerary – Thursday

Ring Tom for briefing　(2)

Input invoices　(1)

Prepare invoices for despatch　(2)

Post　(1)

Outstanding email　(1)

Filing　(1)

Tidy　(1)

Map out appraisal timetable　(3)

Finish report on customer activity　(6)

Compile letter of invitation　(4)

Prep sales training session　(6)

Ring George for update　(1)

Weekly update meeting (10am)　(3)

It doesn't matter at the start if there isn't a logical sequence to the things you have to do, because the second stage is about 'prioritization'. What's far more critical is that you try to capture all the things you need to do today, and get them onto the list with a time frame allocated against them. The number in brackets after each task relates to the projected time needed and each unit represents 10 minutes, so a number 2 means you've given yourself 20 minutes for the task, a 6 represents an hour. Don't let any individual task go over the limit of 6. If you're working on a major project, split it down into hour-long chunks and try to put other tasks in between to 'refresh' you. The other outcome of this is that as you tick off each hour completed, you'll feel as though you've achieved something, and can target yourself more accurately for the next hour.

> 66 99
>
> 'There is no such thing as a long piece of work, except one that you dare not start.'
> Charles Baudelaire
> (French poet)

Deciding on the order of priority is the next task, and this is made much easier once you've got into the habit of accurate day mapping. You will instinctively know where to place tasks, according to the part of the day most suited to them.

Itinerary – Thursday

(12) Ring Tom for briefing   (2)

(10) Input invoices   (1)

(11) Prepare invoices for despatch   (2)

(3) Post   (1)

(2) Outstanding email   (1)

(8) Filing   (1)

(9) Tidy   (1)

(1) Map out appraisal timetable   (3)

(5) Finish report on customer activity   (6)

(7) Compile letter of invitation   (4)

(6) Prep sales training session   (6)

(13) Ring George for update   (1)

(4) Weekly update meeting (10am)   (3)

Down the left hand side of our list there is now a number order for each of the tasks, starting with 'map out appraisal timetable' at number 1, and going through to 'ring George for update' at 13. Each of the tasks is placed into the time of day we allocated to varying activities in our day map, so the high attention tasks are first, followed by creative, then sort and finally people management.

Slotted into the morning is the update meeting at number 4, which, although it is driven by someone else's demands, we have to make room for on our agenda, and work around it the best we can.

The more familiar you become with your day map, the easier it will be to allocate an order of priority to individual tasks, so that they fit in with the pattern you've established for yourself. Think of the process of mapping your day in a series of stages:

♦ List

♦ Cluster

♦ Timings

♦ Targets

Getting everything down on paper is the first part; your day map will help you cluster jobs into the right time slot, but it's also important to put time frames against each task so that you can complete the last stage, which is targeting yourself.

PERTINENT POST-IT

♦ Preparation is an essential part of detox so use these tools and techniques wisely
♦ Fuel is important but hydration is vital
♦ Get to know your own energy curve and use it to devise a personal day map
♦ Test several day maps until you find one which works well for you
♦ Itineraries flow from day maps; use the two in conjunction for maximum effectiveness

NINE

GOOD DETOX BEHAVIOURS

Knowing which tools and techniques will help you, goes part of the way towards making detox easier. But as we've seen in our analysis of the way we work, often the problems we have are caused by the way we behave, so what changes could we make to ensure that our working lives are easier in future?

20 MINUTE BURSTS

Whatever time allocation you've put against the tasks on your itinerary, try to make sure you work for no longer than 20 minutes at a time, before you have some kind of a break. This doesn't involve a cup of tea and a stroll round the car park; it's more of a short pause. Just give yourself a minute off, to stare out of the window or think about what you're having for tea tonight.

This is a great way of controlling your attention span, rather than letting it drift of its own accord. You're much less likely to

'Good things happen when you pay attention.' John F. Smith (American writer)

wander off into another world if you know you've only got a short time before you'll get a 'break'.

If you've tackled a couple of itinerary items that are 10 minutes each (a unit apiece) and you finish early, you can extend your pause as a reward for being ahead of target.

THE POWER HOUR

In conjunction with your 20-minute bursts you can develop your own power hour. For maximum effectiveness, set aside an hour when your energy and attention are at their highest and your likelihood of interruption lowest. If you have a private office, close the door, switch to voicemail and close down your email program.

By doing all of this you are removing the disruptions that are often a part of our 'peripheral vision'; they're the things which distract you from the job in hand.

You don't have to use a 'power hour' every day, just when you have a particular task that needs your full attention. By setting a start and end time, you feel a weight of responsibility to really crack on with what you're doing, so tell yourself you must have this finished by the allotted time and you'll be amazed at how much you can get through.

Power hours are good for achieving set goals, whenever you need them, but they can be even more effective if you use them first thing in the morning, when the office tends to be quieter. To do this, you'll need to be organized the night before, so that when you arrive you can get started straight away, instead of having to tidy up, plan your day, make a coffee etc., etc.

THE RULE OF THREE

On the subject of attention spans, part of keeping your mind de-cluttered is giving yourself the freedom of focussing on a little at a time. Don't make the mistake of looking at your itinerary and worrying about the 26 tasks you have to do today; instead, concentrate on what's on your desk now, and carry a maximum of two more things in your head that need to be done.

This is a manageable enough number not to distract you, but it will help to keep up a level of awareness of what else you have to do. This can be especially important when you're involved in a meeting which has no set end time: thinking about what else is on your desk will make you much more efficient in coming to conclusions, rather than letting it degenerate into a 'talking shop'.

STOPPING

None of us looks forward to conflict and the trouble with 'stopping' doing things that aren't your responsibility is that we fear this is where it'll lead, but it doesn't have to be that way. As well as all the things that were either in your job description or that you've assumed as part of your role through long-standing precedent, there is a very high chance that you have taken on additional duties or responsibilities over time.

This is a natural process of evolution in our jobs and isn't something to be feared or dismissed. If we only ever did what was set for us, then there would be no challenge, nothing to stretch us. The difficulty with this unfolding expansion of our roles is that it is often indiscriminate and organic; it grows over time with no particular logic to it. You might be asked to take on more based on your skills and experience, but all too often it happens because 'there's no one else to do it'. It's quite common too for this kind of delegation to happen in your absence, when you couldn't make a particular meeting, so the other attendees decided to land you with something they didn't want to do.

This happens a lot with issues of compliance; you know the kind of thing: health and safety, diversity policy, corporate social responsibility … is any of this ringing any bells?

It's also true that less weighty subjects may land on your desk, too, which are really nothing to do with your core role. You can, and must, stop doing these things if you are going to successfully detox. You can approach the task in two ways. You can either announce that you are not going to be responsible for this any more, which is brave, but justifiable if you have more important things to be getting on with; or you can simply stop of your own accord.

CASE STUDY – GETTING IT RIGHT IN SCHOOL

Lady Marie Stubbs became notorious for coming out of retirement to take the headship of St George's school in Westminster, London, where former headmaster Philip Lawrence had been tragically killed while trying to protect his pupils. The school had, not surprisingly, performed badly in its OFSTED inspection, and it was the new head teacher's mission to turn it around. When it came to paperwork she claimed that she only dealt with anything that had a direct bearing on the education or welfare of the children in her charge; everything else went into a separate drawer, and if no one had asked about it in 12 months' time, it was binned.

Her stroke of genius here is that she focussed solely and relentlessly on the one core purpose of her role; so in the same way, we need to think about what the point of our business is. In many commercial enterprises today, our reason for being is to serve the customer as this is at the heart of the organization's profitability. So don't get worn down by people who talk grandly of 'diverse stakeholders' and trying to satisfy many vested interests. If you're performing in a way that delivers against the key objective of the company, you can't go far wrong.

'Occasionally when lower priority things don't get done, there's a bit of noise elsewhere in the system, but quite often, nothing happens at all!'
Andy McFarlane (Marketing Director, IBM UK)

The decision of what to stop is still a difficult one, and it will take you time to work it out. Each day during your detox you should make a physical note of the tasks you undertook that added no value to your core purpose (serving the customer or whatever else). Rate them according to the amount of time they steal from you, then set about stopping.

It's not just in education that this kind of brutal prioritization takes place; it's just as necessary in big business.

Stopping is a great tool in helping to put you in control of your time, but it's one that might threaten other members of your team, so you need to be confident that you're doing it (or to be precise, not doing it) for the right reasons. Making grand claims that 'you intend to use your time more effectively for the good of the customer', then getting caught surfing the net for car insurance quotes, isn't going to win you any friends.

ONE TOUCH/TWO TOUCH

The 'one touch principle' has been around for a while, but for the purposes of detox we've updated it. The underpinning theory is that you only ever touch each piece of paper that crosses your desk once. It's a wonderful idea, but virtually impossible to execute, which is why we've added the 'two touch' clause, which can be implemented under particular circumstances.

Take the post for example, how do you handle it when it arrives? Are you similar to Nancy, who describes her 'relationship' with the post in this way?

NANCY SAYS ...

'I know it's silly, but I still look forward to the post arriving on my desk. I suppose it harks back to my childhood when it was associated with something nice, like the arrival of a birthday present; ever the optimist, I always think some lovely surprise awaits me. You'd think I'd have learned by now!

'The first thing I do is have a quick flick through the pile and mentally note all the items that I'm familiar with. You can often tell who's sent what when it's regular post, then take an educated guess over the rest; so you can pretty much always spot a marketing or promotional brochure, an official letter from the government or the taxman. But the third and best type of post is when you have no idea who it's from and it doesn't look boring!

'I do have a strict order, but I always save the mystery post for last.'

Nancy was typical of the sample we studied, but what was more interesting was that in most cases there was very little system associated with what happened once the envelopes were open. Often all the items were randomly stacked in a pile on the desk, with no sense of importance or priority attached to them.

In the case of the post, and with all other items that cross your workspace, deciding to handle them only once (where possible) is a fantastic time saver. Like all the other activities you undertake, make opening the post a positive action, not a 'displacement activity'; deal quickly with as much as you can and add any bigger tasks to your itinerary in the time slot that suits you best. In too many cases, the arrival of the mail is one of the top distractions of the morning, allowing us to break off from what we're doing, with the justification that there might be something urgent or important awaiting us. We'd never admit, like Nancy, that the post gives us the hint of a thrill, because it might contain a nice surprise!

Detox is all about focus, so diverting from one activity to another is to be avoided. The potential urgency of what the post might contain doesn't hold water any more, either. Let's face it, if you wanted someone to act urgently, conventional mail wouldn't be the first method you'd think of to contact them. Much more likely would be an email, or even a phone call.

One touch should be applied to all items (post and otherwise) that are nice to have or simply irrelevant junk (like mailers, flyers, or badly targeted data); decide there and then if there is any relevance to you and if not, bin it.

A 'second (but no more) touch' can be applied to items that will take time to digest and require some action or decision to be undertaken. What this process drives you to do is to make your actions very deliberate and considered. So you never find yourself idly glancing at a report or browsing absent-mindedly through a trade magazine: you're either reading and actioning these things, or you aren't.

Even the best detoxers have their failings and one touch/two touch is perhaps the hardest discipline to master, especially when you apply it beyond the purely physical and act in a similar way with email, too.

How often have you been in the middle of something desperately important and urgent, but have been tempted away from it instantly, by the 'ping-pong' chime of email arriving? This is perhaps the most disruptive and difficult time-stealer of all, because once you've been drawn into the inbox it's hard to escape.

Just look at that list of unread messages, highlighted in bold and containing who knows what. This makes the thrill of the post pale into insignificance; all sorts of pleasures could await you, disguised behind a seemingly innocuous few words in the subject field.

Focus! Stop and think about one touch/two touch with your email and you'll deal with it much more efficiently. This means you have to set time aside for it, just like with the physical letters that arrive each day, and deal with it effectively in one or two decisive passes. Make a point of including some dedicated email-handling time in your itinerary.

TRIVIA MANAGEMENT

You're in the newsagent's trying to decide between the *Guardian* or *Heat* magazine. For the modern, efficient switched-on office worker of today, there's only one choice: much better to buy the quality newspaper and be up to date with the world than mire ourselves in the trivia of celebrities' lifestyles; but when faced with a quiet moment, when nobody will discover our guilty secret, which of us wouldn't sneak a peek to see who the glitterati are dating or which reality 'star' has just re-entered rehab?

We face these choices all the time. Have you ever started a serious session of internet research and ended up playing some daft online game of skittles or 'Beat the goalie'? Consciously diverting your attention to some mindless activity is fine for giving your batteries time to recharge, but make it a managed process, or you'll end up whiling the day away with trivia.

If you're efficiently day-mapping and constructing an itinerary, you can make sure that time is built in for trivia, because it's an important part of maximizing your efficiency, especially when it involves some social interaction with other members of the team. A conversation about last night's telly, a recent football match or a juicy bit of gossip is part of what makes the world go round for most of us.

Part of working effectively is underpinned by the principle that our attention span is limited, especially when we're trying to concentrate really hard. Recognizing this and working in short bursts, during which we can give our maximum attention, followed by even shorter rest periods, will increase the amount you get through.

These tools and techniques of detox are not just critical to its success, but they will also help you drive through the 10-day process with your sanity intact.

PERTINENT POST-IT

◆ Short, sharp shock! Work in 20-minute bursts, stay fo-cussed then take a short break
◆ The power hour is a great way of concentrating all your efforts on a specific task
◆ Don't clutter your mind with lots of tasks; keep to a maxi-mum of three
◆ Stop doing what you don't have to!
◆ Be decisive and deliberate; if you pick something up, action it!
◆ Take frequent breaks; trivia is okay as long as you man-age it

TEN

BEING TIDY

So far, we've looked at the way we live our lives in the Analysis section, resulting in a 'where am I now?' outcome. From there, we've been through a four-stage method of preparation, so that we've got a plan to follow, but what about a support mechanism? We've outlined some tools and techniques, but there's a further key principle for effective detox and it's covered here.

IN PRAISE OF TIDINESS

Imagine what it would be like if you went into your local library, intending to borrow a book by your favourite author, and the librarian assured you that they had it ('I saw it only the other day'), but couldn't be too specific where it was. 'Give me a clue,' you'd say, asking if the books were filed alphabetically by author, arranged by genre or even chronologically according to the date published.

What if they replied, 'Oh no, we don't arrange the books here, we just put them anywhere there's a space, but feel free to have a look around'?

It just wouldn't work, would it?

At the other end of the spectrum, is there any such thing as too tidy? Is it possible to have things too well ordered? Maybe you know someone who files all their music by artist and gets stressed if they find a mistake, or they keep all their kitchen appliances in cupboards (toaster, kettle, the lot) until they're needed.

One of the core principles of detox is to bring order and method to what we do, but there is a limit and that is defined by the cross-over point where additional tidiness ceases to increase our efficiency and becomes our obsession; if it's for its own sake, it's pointless.

So you're entitled to keep questioning yourself during the process of tidying up: is this helping or is it just a bit mad?

Let's say that we all intend to remain the right side of sane during this process. What will help us to get tidy? How can we prepare the ground?

THE ETHOS OF TIDINESS

Ergonomics

This is the study of working conditions, and it looks specifically at the effective utilization of our environment and the design of the equipment we use. It follows that being tidy requires some groundwork in this area if detox is going to be successful.

Just as our work spreads out to fill the time available, so our untidiness seeps into every corner of the space that we're allocated. For this reason, a really good starting point is to imagine what it would be like if that space was slashed to a fraction of its size.

Most of us share the experience of having lived or worked in different-sized spaces. Maybe your parents moved from a small house to a bigger one and, though you all appreciated having a bit more room to breathe, it wasn't as if you couldn't exist at all in the old property; you just had to be a bit more thoughtful.

As well as space, there's the issue of how your storage works. Do you have filing cabinets, folders, box files, shelves, drawers …? There are many alternatives. The tough questions you have to ask yourself when considering ergonomics are: 'Do these facilities function properly?', 'Do they actually help me stay tidy?' and, 'Is there any system or method to the way I use them?'

Minimalization

This can otherwise be defined as 'a good clear-out'! Later, we'll come on to the detail of a healthy chucking-out session, but for now, we're just concentrating on the items that are close to hand. Often, we duplicate certain bits of office equipment when we don't need to. There's something about a visit to the stationery cupboard that can bring out the worst in us. All we've gone for is a pad of lined A4 paper, but once the door is opened, it's like removing the lid from Pandora's box: shiny things catch your eye, tactile items urge you to caress them; before you know it, you're beginning to think just how useful a hole-punch could be to you!

But that's just the start. The next phase is gluttony. Okay, you've already got a blue ballpoint on your desk, but you know how easily they can be lost; you either put it down or someone 'borrows' it … better to get another one while you're here; in fact, pick up three to save you another trip. Oh yes and a red one; you never know when that'll come in handy for highlighting things, and talking of highlighters … It just goes on and on until you've collected at least one of everything, all of it absolutely vital to your existence.

If you're a normal person in their thirties or above, who has worked in an office for 10 years or more, the chances are you haven't got enough of your life left to use up all the ink in all the biros you've accumulated. What is all the more remarkable is that you can still never find one when you want to.

ALAN'S BIRO

'I remember when I was growing up that my dad (Alan), who worked for the Civil Service, had a black biro; I can picture it still. Although it was nothing special to look at, it seemed to write better than any other in the house; it never went all blobby and you didn't have to breathe on it, or score it back and forth for five minutes before the ink started to flow.

'This biro was standard Civil Service issue and to prevent it from 'walking' it was branded with the words 'Government Property', which were actually melted into the plastic.

'When it ran out, dad had to requisition a refill from the Stationery Department (I wonder what he used to write that with?). It once went missing and the house was turned upside down. Each member of the family was quizzed, using techniques that infringed our human rights; that's how important it was.

'It turned up again in the end, but dad had to have many months of "post biro temporary loss trauma syndrome" counselling. To my certain knowledge he only ever used that one biro during thirty years of service.'

So, next time you visit the stationery cupboard – think Alan.

At home

Everything has a place where it rightfully belongs; as humans we think of this as home, but inanimate objects feel the same, too: rubber bands and paper clips, phone chargers, files, diaries, Post-its and project notes – in fact the desk-detritus that surrounds us all. Every single one of these items belongs somewhere and in not allowing it to return there you are indulging in a kind of cruelty: it really wants to go home.

One of the great difficulties, for all of us, is that if we move away from home for long enough and spend time in different places for extended periods, we start to lose our sense of where home is. Maybe the same is true for the paperclips: it's so long since they resided in that special little compartment in the desk tidy that sits in your top drawer (now occupied by grit, some pencil shavings and a very sticky cough sweet) that they don't even think of it as home any more. Instead, they're lost in their nomadic existence, occasionally linking up with a friend on the surface of your desk, but more often than not, tucked away out of sight under a coffee mug.

There will be plenty of items that have made their home on the surface of your desk, but no matter how frequently you use them, they need to be moved, out of sight, to a new home.

We'll return to this principle later, when we get into the detox programme, but for now it's worth thinking about all the accumulated bits and pieces on your desk and its surrounding environs. Consider where it all came from and, for that matter, where it's all about to go back to. To quote a very old fashioned saying, 'a place for everything and everything in its place'.

'Wipe as you go'

Sometimes you see this sign in restaurant kitchens, and it's a good rule to borrow when you're detoxing.

Even very small tasks, if allowed to accumulate because you've left them undone, can eventually become a mountain to climb; whereas, if you're constantly on top of them, they are only ever a single small task. Apply this rule rigorously to your workspace.

A domestic example of how untidiness can become endemic is the washing-up. Even as a single person living in your own space, you seem to generate an enormous amount of it, especially if you ever cook or bake anything from scratch. There's nothing quite so frustrating as trying to stack a new load of clean dishes on a rack that already contains the contents of the last bowlful. On the contrary, there is nothing so satisfying as coming down to breakfast to find a clean and tidy kitchen. Apply 'wipe as you go' to the washing-up and see how tidy it makes you. Apply it to your desk and you'll reduce your stress.

Consciousness

If you ever sit at your desk at your workplace, staring out of the window, while little birds flutter and tweet inside your head, then you are perfectly normal, but you are also semi-conscious. If your boss catches you in this state, be sure to make the point that this is the expression on your face when you're being creative. Indeed, you can even make a virtue of it: 'Sorry about that, you just caught me blue-skying!'

The reality might well be that this activity is your deliberate attempt to de-stress. On the other hand you might just be bored; but whatever the reason, it illustrates how quickly we can lapse into a 'state of not noticing'. During this time, it's easy to lose a grip on your system of detox, so whatever your best intentions may have been, you now find yourself sitting in front of a messy desk once more.

The danger zone is when you stop noticing your untidiness. It's not worth panicking about, but it helps if it raises your awareness. This consciousness is vital for a good detox and sustained success.

Splurge

Best intentions are all well and good, but there are times when mess is an absolute necessity (as long as it's conscious mess). Probably, for most of us, this is when we're being creative. It would be hard to redecorate a room in your house without causing any mess, but we take precautions.

We remove the furniture, pack away the knick-knacks (they could probably do with a good detox too, but let's not worry about that now), then cover everything else with dust sheets; after that, we don our old clothes and make a start. If we've got any sense of organization at all, we set aside a short period of time in which to complete the task, and at the end, we clear everything up with one massive 'splurge'.

The same can happen at work; as long as you know you're in for a messy time (intellectually, we presume, not actually), you can make some provision for it. When the task is complete, and the area looks like a bomb has hit it, a good splurge will get you back to normal again.

The tidiness part of detox can seem a bit intense, but it's all a matter of attitude. If you're doing it for its own sake you're on the wrong side of efficient and have lapsed into obsession. If you've undertaken it for the right reasons, however, there's a purpose to it all and it doesn't seem mad in the slightest. Nevertheless, the process can be quite exhausting, especially when you're not used to it, so think about the elements of the method that we've outlined here, employ them with vigour, but then allow yourself time to relax a bit; not only will you deserve it, but you'll have the time to do it too and that really is the whole point.

If you need to remind yourself of the key reasons to stay on top of things, the following list will help.

TEN TOP TIDINESS TIPS:

Being tidy:

◆ De-clutters your mind
◆ Means not having to remember where everything is
◆ Saves time
◆ Makes you look more efficient
◆ Speeds up your work rate
◆ Allows you to focus on the job in hand
◆ Increases your sense of purpose
◆ Reduces stress
◆ Facilitates creative thinking
◆ Feels good!

PERTINENT POST-IT

- ◆ A place for everything and everything in its place!
- ◆ Stay conscious of your surroundings and it will help you keep tidy
- ◆ Stationery is your friend, but you can have too much of a good thing!
- ◆ A little and often is a good principle for keeping tidy
- ◆ If it gets out of hand sometimes, don't panic; splurge!

ELEVEN

FINAL DETOX THOUGHTS

Be aware, before you start your detox, that some of the actions you'll be asked to take might seem like trivial ones. That really is the whole point of the programme: its success hangs on *not* taking up hours of your time.

You might also like to stop and consider that *'intent is the antithesis of action'. Meaning* to keep your workspace clear, sort out the filing, tidy your desk drawers, or whatever else it is you've set for yourself, is not the same as *actually doing it,* and under most circumstances the energy you waste by having these tiny things left undone is much greater than the effort it takes to do them. The world doesn't end if you go home, leaving your desk looking like a bomb has hit it, but on bad days (and we all have them) the extra effort it takes to find the file you're looking for or the frustration of a jammed stapler are hard to keep in context. Possibly you have witnessed the ludicrous sight of a work colleague swearing at an inanimate object, only to find that this does very little to remedy the situation.

Most of the 'stuff' we use in our daily working lives, the equipment that is supposed to enable us, is fit for purpose at first. If you don't

'Begin somewhere. You cannot build a reputation on what you *intend* to do.' Liz Smith (American journalist)

keep it that way, it will come back to bite you, which, in the case of jammed staplers, nearly always results in bloodshed!

You might recall that earlier we referred to the daily energy cycle that we all go through, and this is bound to have an effect on our mood: the lower you're feeling, the less efficient your coping mechanisms will be, so even quite minor mishaps can be blown out of all proportion.

To make the very most of your high-energy time, make sure you tidy up each night before you go home. It's the right sign-off to a good day's work, and it means that you won't be faced with a mess when you arrive in the morning, which is something that would guarantee a bad start to a new day.

Try not to lose momentum half way through, either on an individual task or the detox programme as a whole, as the chances are that you'll look back and wonder why you bothered. We all do this; set off at a run to achieve something new, and then falter along the course. Maybe you pledged to learn a new language before visiting a foreign country for the first time; you listen intently to the tapes, repeating phrases like 'La plume de ma tante' only to run out of steam (or motivation) after a week or two. When you land on distant shores, the time you took at the start is a complete waste unless you followed it through to the point where you could string a few useful sayings together, like 'Can you direct me to the nearest post office?' and 'Please tell me where to find the coldest beer in town.'

Have you ever started the washing-up at home, only to give up halfway through the 'putting away' stage? There you go, then.

Concentration and focus are imperative, too. You are used to using both when trying to decipher the important points in a report that's landed on your desk, mainly because you know that reading it once, properly, is much more efficient than scanning it several times, not taking in the key points.

GUILT AND GOAL-SETTING

Rabbi Lionel Blue has been a regular contributor to Radio 4's *Thought for the Day* over many years, but in addition to his broadcasting exploits he also occasionally tours small theatres, talking about his faith and the beliefs of others. During a question and answer session, he was called on to define which was the stronger: Catholic or Jewish guilt. After some debate he called it a tie, adding that 'neither religion should take pride in engendering it, because no matter what you believe in, guilt carries no positive attributes'.

When it comes to your detox, the aim should be to replace 'guilt' with 'realism'.

As in so many areas of our lives, this detox will involve some goal-setting, either formally or implicitly, if you're trying to achieve something. You will need to know what success looks like, which by necessity drives some measures into the process.

Similarly we might do this with our houses or gardens, promising ourselves we'll keep them tidy; with our relationships with our partners, we'll work to stay romantic; with our children, we'll try to be a good father or mother. But an ongoing cause of dissatisfaction for many of us is that we don't manage to sustain these behaviours in the long term.

If you take a zero-tolerance approach to detox, then the aim is to have everything 100% right for 100% of the time, and the reason for this is that high aspiration is the only way to deliver tangible results. For example, you never hear anyone say, 'I've decided to be a good parent to my children, but only on the days when I can be bothered.' So, stretching yourself is a good thing. It can also be a cause of great dissatisfaction, if you let it.

'If success is doing everything on your to-do list, more often that not you will fail.'
Andy McFarlane (Marketing Director, IBM UK)

The truth is that it's not just unrealistic, it's positively unhealthy to get to 100%. If everything in your life was at that level, what would be the point of carrying on? We need an achievement gap to drive us, so having one shouldn't make us feel guilty.

We talked earlier about our natural tendency to focus on the things we *haven't* yet achieved, rather than be proud of what we have. Aim for 100%, be satisfied with 80% and look forward to tackling the remaining 20% tomorrow, because it will always be there waiting for you; it's instrumental in your sense of purpose, it's part of life.

Don't fall into the trap of thinking that you've under-achieved. Look instead at how far you've come and imagine the gap as the challenge ahead.

Handling change

Understanding who we are, and what our attitude to change is, is the first step to being able to alter the way we behave, the way we think and act.

Sometimes we find it hard to own up, even to ourselves, about what drives us, because we might find something we don't like and not want to admit to it. Often, people blame those around them for not achieving everything they want. You must have heard someone talking about all the things they *could* have done, if it wasn't for so and so: 'Well, I'd have travelled the world, if it wasn't for my partner's parochial attitude.' Often, the truth is that the partner acts as an excuse, so that we don't have to admit that we're afraid to travel the world, or fulfil some other ambition.

We all present a face to other people that we want them to see, a version of ourselves. Sometimes, if they are a good judge of character, they see through this and get a feel for what *really* drives us. If they're truly insightful, they might understand more about us than we do ourselves; they're the people who are able to predict our behaviour in any given

'I'm not scared of change; I'm scared of being bored. I hate to stay still because life is too short and there are too many new things, but many people are afraid of being outside of their comfort zone. They think of all the things that might go wrong. I imagine the worst outcome and think of what I would do. Once you've got a solution, nothing is so bad. It actually works and puts you back in control.' Lynn Rutter (Consultant, Organization Development, Oxfam)

situation. They often make good counsellors, because they're able to suggest to us reasons why we might act in a certain way, under particular circumstances, and give us the chance to reflect on our behaviour.

When neither we, nor they, can predict an outcome in a particular situation, we are into the area of *unknown*. With all of us there are things we are yet to discover about ourselves, and we present no outward signs of what this might be (after all, it's unknown!). On this basis, even the most insightful of people won't be able to foretell the future, but this is the area where our *potential* lies.

As far as our detox is concerned, it's this 'unknown' area which is of greatest significance, for the simple reason that we're trying to change the established patterns of our lives. If you've opted to detox because you're fed up with being cluttered and disorganized, then these are two characteristics you already know are a part of you. That's the easy bit. What is much harder is to uncover the things that have remained hidden up until now, but this is where your future potential lies. By raising our level of consciousness over what we do and how we behave, through completing the detox programme, we're much better placed to uncover some of these unknowns; then we can take decisions about how, and if, we want to change.

Change, trying something new if you like, is both scary and exciting for most of us, and in adult life we often feel more inclined to change incrementally so as to stay in control. Substantial overnight changes in others make us suspicious, as we're aware that for us to do likewise would require an earth-shaking cataclysm. You may have witnessed someone losing a lot of weight or changing their entire wardrobe very suddenly and, cynicism aside, we often discover that this is a result of a new relationship, or the failure of a well-established one; men who are old enough to know better are supposed to go out and buy sports cars or a Harley Davidson if their marriage is failing!

The upside of change is that it can be tremendously exciting and energizing. Often we feel stale within our daily existence, following the same routine. Safe it may be, but dynamic it's not, and as human beings we often crave the wind of change as a form of thrill-seeking.

It's also true that while we present ourselves to the world in one way, none of us likes to be pigeon-holed by a single set of values; we all have a sneaky desire to shock now and again. Maybe the grey-suited clerical worker resents being seen as staid and is just waiting for the right moment to boast to his colleagues that he indulges in extreme sports every weekend.

Detox is about change, so to supplement the formal programme we've introduced an additional challenge for every day, so that while you're in this frame of mind, you have the opportunity for a bit of 'controlled reinvention'.

If you're naturally suspicious of the kind of people who seem to be forever swapping metaphorical horses, politically, spiritually or just fashion-wise, then take heart in the promise that these changes are suggested for trial purposes, but they're for you to control. You can adopt, adapt or reject each one, but only after you've tried them out for yourself.

The connection between these seemingly unrelated alterations in taste or behaviour and your detox is that you have the opportunity over the 10-day period to explore areas of yourself that up until now might have been hidden.

The longer-term purpose, beyond giving you the opportunity to experience some new things, is to illustrate through action that change is something you're in control of, and that scheduling changes into your life, in a conscious way, can make for an exciting time ahead.

At the start of every day, there is something new to try, though your first element of control over these new behaviours is that you don't have to follow them in the order stated. Just be aware that, even if you alter this, it's important to still undertake one a day, and to complete all the suggestions by the end of your detox. You can read ahead if you want to find out what's in store; this will be especially helpful for the changes that require a bit of advance preparation and the bonus is that you can look forward to some of the new things you're going to be trying.

 PERTINENT POST-IT

◆ Intent is the antithesis of action; *meaning* to do something isn't the same as doing it

◆ The energy taken worrying about something not done is greater than the effort it takes to do it

◆ Aim high, but however far you get, be proud of your achievements

◆ There will always be things that are left undone; accept it and move on

◆ Change can be exciting and energizing

◆ Reduce your 'fear factor' by taking control

◆ Keep a note of the new things you uncover about yourself

TWELVE

READY STEADY GO!

This is it, then. You've studied the analysis section, thought hard about how and why we live (and work) the way we do and considered the methods we can use to detox our desks.

The good news is that detox starts here. Well, almost.

If we haven't emphasized it enough, preparation is the key to success, so before you embark on day one, there are a few final checks to be made, to help you through the coming 10 days. The reason so many of our good intentions come to nothing is that we don't recognize just how good we are or how far we've travelled. Our natural human tendency is to focus on how much is still to be done, rather than to reflect on the benefit of the steps we've taken.

Can you remember what it was like when you moved into a new home? In the first few days we make a note, either physically or, more usually mentally, of all the things we're going to achieve, all the changes we're going to make. We'll decorate this room, change the layout of the garden, get rid of that fireplace, buy new door furniture – a whole host of alterations both big and small.

Twelve months later, you look around and let's say you managed to do 75% of the things on your list, the focus of your attention will still be the 25% left undone. Worse than this, during the course of the year, you'll have added tasks to your list as you've uncovered them (replace the guttering, board and light the loft, re-organize the shed, it goes on and on), all of which increases our dissatisfaction as the 'undone' jobs multiply and the 'done' ones pale into insignificance.

To add insult to injury, the positive changes we've made, soon become 'business as usual'. So if you've decorated a room, you're stunned by the improvement when you walk in, at least for the first two weeks. After that, you occasionally congratulate yourself on a job well done, but six months later, it's just part of your living space. You take it for granted.

Apply this principle to all the achievements in your life, and pretty soon it'll seem like you never made much impact at all. This was never more so than on the occasions when other people are chipping away at your self-esteem. If you've ever lost your job, this next story will ring a few bells.

REDUNDANCY AND THE BUCKET OF WATER THEORY

'When I look back, I suppose I brought a lot of misery on myself. I'd always worked hard, or so I thought, so when I was made redundant, out of the blue, I was very bitter indeed. It was around that time that I came up with this bucket of water theory. I developed this metaphor where the organization I'd worked for was represented by a bucket of water. When I joined it, I put my hand in the bucket.

'When I lost my job, I took my hand out then and studied the bucket. It hadn't changed by a single drop in the time that I'd been there; my impact had been nil, my contribution worthless. I was just one of a group of people who dipped in and out of the bucket over a period of time and none of us made a jot of difference.

'I couldn't see that, for the time I was there, I'd swooshed my hand around, made some waves, altered the temperature, moved the bucket a bit and that when I left, there remained a bit of me – a memory, a bit of my DNA if you like – which, although it felt like it was soon forgotten, was part of the make-up of the bucket, at least for a time.'

So, you can see that the impact we make can easily go unnoticed; and the greatest culprit of all in this is ourselves, if we fail to recognize what we've done.

With the process of detox, it's important that this doesn't happen, or you just lose heart and revert back to your old ways. You might find that all that early effort had no lasting positive effect.

REFLECTION

Humans are notoriously bad at accurate reflection; very poor at being able to recall detail; and very suggestible when it comes to doing so. In fact, many of our earliest memories can often turn out to be influenced by what we subsequently hear of events from members of our family. This so called 'inherited memory' is often based on what we've been *told* happened, rather than on our actual recollection.

In the same way, as we mature we often see our past, either through 'rose-tinted spectacles' ('remember the good old days'), or as much bleaker than it really was. A 'spiritualist', who gained a good deal of credence in the Eighties, started every one-to-one discussion by saying, 'I can see a lot of sadness in your life over the last ten years,' to which the respondent would nod sadly and agree. You don't have to stop and think about it for too long to realize that over any 10-year period of anyone's life there will have been 'downs' as well as 'ups'. The so-call spiritualist's trick was to leave this sadness open to interpretation, so for some, it could be the loss of a relative (grandparents have a habit of not going on forever) or it might have been something less significant, like the death of a family pet or a lost love; under such circumstances, it's all too easy for us to focus on the bad things. The truth is that our memories are poor and tend towards the negative. Make a conscious effort to counterbalance this with positive recollections.

RECORDING

So that you'll be able to establish the amount of progress you make during your detox, there are three things that you will need to audit and record before you start on day one.

Space

Take time to log everything that populates your personal work-space, including your desk and any ancillary filing, either in separate cabinets or box files. The best way of doing this is with a digital camera. A dozen photos should be sufficient to capture what's on the surface of your desk, what the drawers contain and the general operating environment you inhabit. Usually, images that remain on your computer end up being forgotten; it's much more significant if you print out a hard copy, so you actually have something to hold. If you don't have access to a camera, draw a picture of your desktop and label it up with everything that's on it, then make a list of what's in the drawers and cupboards. This will work but it's not as powerful as seeing the actual images.

Input and output

Using the picture overleaf as a guide, list the inputs and outputs in the appropriate arrows, saying where each individual task comes from, and where it goes after you've processed it. This starts out as an easy procedure, but once you've used up the physical elements, like the invoice or the information request, you'll need to start thinking about the more intangible aspects of your working day, such as the times when you're called on to exercise your creativity to help solve a problem. Either way, all of this needs to be recorded, because otherwise you'll start with a clean workspace, but it will soon get trashed as the traffic of work starts to flow through it.

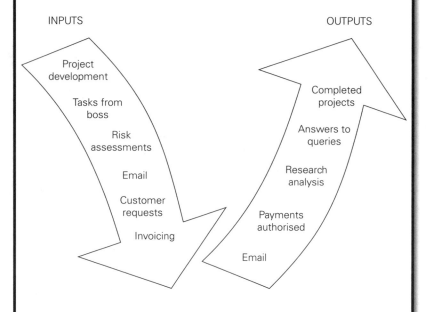

INPUTS

Project development

Tasks from boss

Risk assessments

Email

Customer requests

Invoicing

OUTPUTS

Completed projects

Answers to queries

Research analysis

Payments authorised

Email

The time cake

The amount of difficulty you will experience during detox will very much be governed by the way you manage your time. If, like many managers, you spend a lot of your day fire-fighting, you will never feel like you can spare the time to stay 'clean'. The 'time cake' here is split fairly evenly, but yours might not be; with routine jobs, try to fit them into the part of your day map that suits your working style; sideline the boring things by remembering to 'wipe as you go' so that they never build up to a significant degree.

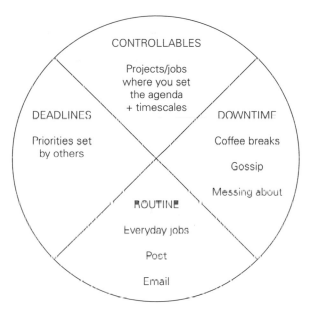

Put controllable tasks in their own time slot and try whenever possible to make sure they aren't 'bumped out' by other people's deadlines. As long as you're being reasonable, you can 'negotiate' when people want things by, but in order to do so, you have to present them with a rationale as to why, and if you've got scheduled tasks (even if they are self-scheduled), this gives some weight to your argument.

'When I'm involved in client-related activities people understand that I'm not likely to get round to what they've asked me for. Because we're very client driven, they're very forgiving.'
Andy McFarlane (Marketing Director, IBM UK)

The time cake recognizes that you will have some downtime, not in itself a bad thing, because we all need periods in which to re-charge our batteries; just be careful it doesn't start to encroach on the whole cake!

JOB ANALYSIS

In lots of jobs, no two days are the same, so what you're attempting to do is find a mean average of activity, say over a week or two. Make three lists, headed 'solo', 'delegated' and 'group'. In each of the columns, write down the major activities you undertake, then estimate the rough percentages of each over a day. The definitions of the three categories are as follows:

1   'Solo' incorporates all the activity you undertake as part of your job. You don't need anyone to tell you on a daily basis that it needs to be done; in fact, it's pretty much routine. If you're the key-holder, and it's up to you to open the shop each day, then that qualifies as a solo activity. As well as

designated tasks, there will be a series of methods you use, some of which will have been laid down by protocol (e.g. handed down to you by the person who used to do the job) and some you will have 'invented' yourself, either because it makes your life easier, or because, through diligence, you have determined that it makes the quality of your output better.

2   'Delegated' refers to the things that other people give you to do, and although this will usually be your direct boss, in freer thinking organizations, the entire management team may have some jurisdiction over your working day. These things are less routine, but may not be entirely one-off, so although you can't incorporate them into your solo definition, they may still be a regular part of what you do.

3   'Group activities', like meetings, for example, may be regular, and might take up a lot of your time. What can be even more intrusive are the *ad hoc* events that take place in response to an unfolding situation, like a crisis meeting to discuss budget shortfalls, or a planning exercise in support of a sales drive.

Use your own time cake to log where you are now, and repeat the exercise at the end of the detox, as a way of measuring how much *control* you have over your working day.

You will have the opportunity to accurately measure your progress against all these criteria at the end of the detox process. When that happens, stay positive about what you've achieved, and use the results as a springboard to spur you on to even better levels of efficiency.

In this final chapter before the start of the detox, we've had the chance to take a deep breath and think about the current state of play. In raising our consciousness and recording an accurate 'picture', we have set a benchmark, which we'll be able to use later to judge the success of the programme.

PERTINENT POST-IT

◆ Human nature leads us to focus on negatives – break this habit

◆ Keeping an accurate log of your starting point will act as a measure for the journey you've travelled on

◆ Don't get obsessed by the things you haven't done; congratulate yourself on your progress to date instead

◆ Become conscious of the tasks other people give you and assess your overall level of control

◆ Be prepared to 'negotiate' over what you accept or reject, but make sure you have a sound rationale

THE DETOX PROGRAMME

THIRTEEN

DAY ONE

Week one

This is the start of your daily detox programme. Each day will begin with a 'change of the day' for you to consider, and there will be three further actions to take, usually along a theme. These actions build over the course of the two week programme, each adding a little to your detox.

We've talked about the importance of having time to reflect on your actions, so each day before you go home, take a minute to think about what's happened and record your thoughts in a Daily Detox Journal.

As preparation is the key to success in so many of our work-based activities, most days will involve you thinking about and planning what is to follow in the morning. This shouldn't be too difficult and often you will be able to complete your prep on the way home, just by considering what the next day will hold.

CHANGE OF THE DAY

Go for a walk. If you'd normally do this anyway, then alter your route so that you discover something new. If it's not a normal part of your routine, you'll need to think about where you're going and when. First thing in the morning can be terrifically energizing, but, equally, an after-work stroll can help to de-stress you; a further option is last thing at night, which gives you a chance to reflect on the day and consider what went well.

The physical exercise you're taking is important, but just as significant is what you do with your *mind* when you're walking. Have you ever witnessed someone walking their dog and talking on their mobile phone at the same time? This clearly defeats the object: if you've gone for a relaxing stroll, to be diverted by either work or some other aspect of your life means that you're missing the point. Your walk today is partly about getting things in context. You're lucky if you live in the country, because the 'force of nature' is all around you, but even if you're a city dweller, there are many things to marvel at which we don't normally take the time to see.

Do your best to clear your mind of the usual pressures that preoccupy you; forget about work and paying the bills, and picture yourself as just another small part of the universe. Thinking about this vastness can make us feel tiny in the overall scheme of things, but at the same time it is a fantastic way of putting any troubles we have into perspective.

Make a real effort to carry the benefit of this with you, because the problems we face are, in reality, very small; it's our *percep-*

tion of them that makes them an issue. If you can maintain a healthy perspective on this then you are much more likely to achieve what you set out to do.

If you didn't wake up this morning with a slight feeling of excitement then you're just not doing it right. Today is the start of a new way of working, a new design for life, which will make you more efficient and effective; who knows where this could lead? – maybe a promotion, or it could simply be that you'll go home on time with the satisfaction that you did a great day's work.

Remembering the daily energy cycle that each of us goes through is important as you prepare to embark on your detox. The reason is that you will need energy and resolve if you're going to be successful. Have you ever started to have a clear-out at home when you've been feeling a bit lacking in energy? What usually happens is that you come across a drawer full of bitty things or a box of photographs and soon become absorbed by the contents rather than focussed on the task. It becomes hard to make 'eject' decisions; in the end you elect to keep everything, but just straighten it up a little. The exercise is completely pointless because detox is about freedom, and you can only achieve that if you're prepared to 'let go' of the detritus that drags you down.

ACTION 1

Before you leave the house, drink half a pint of cold, fresh tap-water; set a reminder on your watch or phone so that it beeps at lunchtime and at 5 p.m. to alert you to do the same thing on both subsequent occasions.

This is all part of feeling good and staying alert; there's an increasing body of evidence that suggests many of us are permanently dehydrated, and studies in schools have shown that children have lower attention spans if they're in this state. Setting the reminder will force you to think consciously about this action for today, but after that, it's up to you to sustain it because, when we're changing habits, our motivation is much stronger if we 'learn' the benefits for ourselves.

ACTION 2

When you arrive at work, make a conscious effort to break with your early morning routine. If you start the day with a coffee, don't; if you ease yourself in gently with a chat, don't. Apart from the need to make this a different day, there is an overriding necessity during your detox to be aware of everything you do and the enemy of active consciousness is routine. Carry on doing things the same way and soon you achieve 'autopilot' status, the kind of dreamy state that most of us live our lives in, the one where we stop questioning what we do and just do it.

Instead, go straight to your workstation. Before you sit down, take a deep breath and survey the scene with a critical and objective eye (you can use two if it helps).

ACTION 3

The first thing to tackle in the process of detoxing your desk is your desk! Most people's desks contain a combination of three elements, which can be categorized as 'personal', 'work' and 'rubbish'. All sorts of things fall into the rubbish category, from the bits of Blu-Tack or bent paperclips you mindlessly play with while on the phone, through to chocolate wrappers, credit card receipts or Post-it notes (whose noteworthy value ceased long ago).

'Personal' also has a variety of guises; mostly it's comprised of photographs of loved ones, maybe even your spouse! Occasionally it might turn out to be some lovingly crafted artefact from a younger member of the family, often constructed of clay or raffia, the kind of material that sheds bits of itself over time. Reminders of 'happier times' are a popular favourite, like images of holidays or of a windswept beach with the dog – we even came across a fully reconstructed beach, housed in an upturned shoebox lid, complete with sand, shells and plastic figures, which really is going a bit too far.

Everything else falls into the work category, so folders and files are part of the picture, but so too is the 'equipment' that allows you to function. Common hardware includes computer keyboards and monitors, but also calculators, desk diaries, clocks, pen-holders and desk-tidies (which are a contradiction in terms).

The first part of the clearing process is to take everything off the desk (except things that might be 'hard-wired' like monitors and keyboards). You can put it all into a box, sort out a drawer to store it temporarily or make some neat piles on the floor around you. As you go, recognize the rubbish for what it is and bin it; if there are re-usable resources (like the Blu-Tack, for example), you need to find a place for them, so put them back with the unused stuff that's hiding in a packet in your drawer. This is the only bit of 'sorting' that needs to be done at this stage, so if it takes you more than 10 minutes, you must be doing something wrong.

Next, you need to think about today. Check your diary and your memory for what needs to be done and write down a list of the files, folders or other paperwork you're going to need, then carefully select them from the pile.

Everything else, unsorted rubbish, personal stuff and work-that's-not-relevant-to-today stays in one place (you might find an old A4 copying paper box a handy tool). You're nearly done now; all that remains is for you to complete your 'day map' for instructions, then put everything you've selected from the box as critical for today's tasks in one place, any place, but most definitely not back on the desk (in a separate drawer maybe).

By now you might be thinking this is a bit of a palaver, but it's far from that. In these simple steps (that should have taken no longer than half an hour at the most) you have cleared your desk completely in preparation for what will 'flow through' during the day, you've made a plan for how to use your time with a day map and you've developed a method of monitoring what's needed and what isn't in an average day. If you're left wondering about that last one, it's as simple as this: everything you thought you were going to use today is in one place. If things change or you hadn't anticipated the need for one file or another, you'll have to go to your 'box' to get it, but as you do, your consciousness will be raised and it's much more likely as you go through this process each day, that you'll get better and better at selecting what's needed.

And just in case you're becoming concerned that you're now dragging a box of miscellaneous stuff around with you, don't worry; over the next few days you'll find a series of instructions on how to solve this temporary situation. In fact, one of the critical elements in making this detox successful is to take it a stage at a time, and to try and make sure that no single set of tasks takes too long; otherwise you'll fill your day with detoxing and get fired for not doing your job.

RETROSPECTIVE

Detoxing is a learning process. You are literally learning a new series of habits, a revised routine to improve your efficiency, and, in order to do that effectively, there needs to be a bit of time set aside each day to reflect on what's happened.

Take 10 minutes out before you go home to think about a couple of things. Firstly, how did you feel this morning about the process of detoxing and has that changed through the day? What might have altered your opinion and can you make things better tomorrow?

Next, look around you; what's different about your workspace now? How has it altered from the way it was when you arrived? Make a mental note of what's better and what's worse, and think of how you might improve your personal space. Tomorrow, what action can you take?

JOURNAL

Record this information in your Daily Detox Journal in whatever your personal style is; you could write a paragraph or just some bullet points. Resist the temptation to find fault, but stop and consider instead one thing that you might do differently if you had the day over again. Was this within your control or might you have to influence someone else? What needs to happen for you to be able to do this?

Now record the way you feel about the day as a whole by writing down three descriptive words, like 'motivated' or 'energized'. These 'feelings' will be an important part of your overall reflection from the programme, so make an effort to record them each day.

PREP

We know by now that just drifting along is no way to really get things done. If you're going to make a success of this detox, you need to stop and think about what it is you want to achieve. Detox breaks this down into usable chunks, so most days, when the main working part of the day is over, there'll be some preparation tasks to complete, so that you're ready to start afresh in the morning.

Again this is a consciousness-raising exercise to make sure that we're not just making the work expand to fit the time. If your contracted hours are nine to five, your objective is to work within this. Many office workers are used to working much longer hours and their working day runs over as a matter of course, but tomorrow you're going home on time!

Your prep today is to think about the hours you're supposed to work, because that's the timing you're going to try and stick to tomorrow.

FOURTEEN

DAY TWO

 CHANGE OF THE DAY

'You are what you eat.' It's a pretty frightening thought when you look at the average western diet! Food is important in many ways; at a base level it is the fuel that sustains us throughout the working day, but the reality is that it is our attitude to food which is much more significant.

Today's changes are threefold. Hydration comes first. There are plenty of sideways references to this during the detox programme, but today try to concentrate extra hard on having enough fluid. Many of us drink lots of tea and coffee during a working day, but water is the best (and cheapest) solution. Try mixing a splash of cordial or fruit juice for flavour, in between your intake of pure water. A little and often is better than bingeing, so keep a bottle with a sports cap on your desk, right in front of you. Make up whatever 'mixers' you fancy the night before and refrigerate them, then keep them chilled in work if you have a fridge nearby (most places do).

Secondly, there's 'change'. Mostly, we eat the same things time and again; in fact, recent surveys have found that as few as six staple meals are served over and over in some households. Your mission today is to try three 'different' foods and we're starting, for the sake of convenience, by recommending fruit. Buy three pieces of fruit that you wouldn't normally eat. This isn't difficult to do, as most supermarkets now stock such a vast variety that you're spoiled for choice. As the detox programme goes on, you can incorporate this action into your weekly shop, aiming to try three new foods a week.

Our fruit recommendation is unashamedly healthy, so your third task is to eat something indulgent; that shouldn't be too hard to do.

What you buy is up to you – cake, chocolate, expensive cheese – it's a matter of taste; the important thing is *when* you eat it. Keep your 'guilty secret' at home, stored out of temptation's way and make a point of setting aside 10 minutes in the evening to enjoy it. Instead of grazing as you pass, or munching in front of the telly, take all other distractions out of the way and savour the moment (and the food), enjoying it for its own pleasure.

This is your reward for today's detox, and it should rightly make you feel good about what you've achieved.

Changes in the detox programme are incremental, so we won't ask you to do everything all of the time. Yesterday was the starting point, the nuts and bolts of simply being tidier and more organized. What we didn't do was attempt, at the same time, to change the shape of your working day. That is a large part of the programme, but the actions are interwoven with other approaches, too.

Your prep for today was to consider your contracted hours and work towards completing your tasks within them. Keep this in mind when you're undertaking the following actions.

ACTION 1

On day one, you filled a box with the contents of your desktop, only taking out the essentials to complete your work. As you did yesterday morning, start by reviewing your work area. It will help if you do this while you're drinking half a pint of fresh tap-water.

Don't sit down until you've completed this process of storing an image of your workspace. It's critically important to be able to look back and see (in your mind's eye) the difference you have made.

Think about any items that crept back onto your desk inadvertently. Hopefully, this won't include any rubbish; if it does then clear this off before you start. More likely there will be work items, either 'live' e.g. something you were actually dealing with, or possibly some of the equipment you use to carry this out (a stray stapler or pad of Post-it notes).

Before you do anything else, put it all in the box, or where you've now decided it belongs. Even if you already know that the first file of the day that you'll 'pull' is the one in front of you, it's critical to start with a completely clear space every day.

ACTION 2

Produce a day-map and itinerary to as high a level of accuracy as is achievable in a 10-minute time slot; remember to allocate task-times as well as prioritizing the order of things to do. Often our itineraries look easy to fulfil, but we frequently get to the end of the day with items left undone; this shows how much time gets 'stolen' from us by other people each day.

Whatever happens today you need to be both relentless and ruthless: your task is to stay focused and to leave work at the time you agreed with yourself when doing your prep last night. To assist your determination, take a Post-it or small piece of paper, draw a clock face on it and show the time of departure, then attach this to the frame of your computer screen, so that every time you look up, you will have a reminder of the necessity to crack on. The last thing you will do tonight, before you leave, is take the clock off the screen and put it in the bin.

ACTION 3

It's time to tackle the box and it's not as daunting as it might sound. If people around you are starting to think your change in behaviour is a little strange, it's nothing in comparison to what they'll feel if you continue to live your life out of a cardboard carton.

As it was only yesterday that you put everything in there, you should still be able to remember roughly what the contents are; now all you need to do is think of categories like files, equipment, personal photos, mementos (hopefully, no full-mock-ups of beaches).

Remove all the work-related things and find a home for them. Don't spend too long doing this or you'll get drawn into re-arranging the entire filing system. Though we're not very keen on 'temporary homes' because they result in taking another decision further down the line, we're big advocates of expediency, which means that it's better to get on and do this quickly, rather than hijack your entire day with a massive reorganization.

The next part of the process involves desk-mapping, which we first introduced in the Method section earlier. It simply means that the greater the frequency of use, the nearer at hand something is. Organize your desk drawers in this way, keeping pens, paper clips and other commonly used stationery in the top drawer. Other items, maybe envelopes, drawing pins, packs of spare staples and refills, go further down.

Sort live and pending files by order of priority, the most urgent at the top, and use another drawer for these.

Any other files or supporting material, like research reports or trade magazines, need a new home; away from your desk, but within easy reach.

Beside the inevitable equipment that was on your desk (which should now be consigned to a desk drawer), you should be able to sort the paperwork into two piles, called 'action' and 'filing'. The filing one doesn't matter too much because once it's put in its proper place, all the evidence points to the fact that it will remain untouched again forever. Calculations have been made (by people who should get out more) on the percentage of files ever referred to again, but this is missing the point: the *amount* isn't the important thing; the real reason we hang onto all this stuff is that we *don't know which* file might be needed again. Don't stress too much over this right now, as we're going to come back to the exciting world of filing on another day – bet you can't wait.

The 'action' pile you've made is important; this can be further sub-divided according to *when* you are going to do it. No, not when you vaguely think you'll get round to it, not all in a single pile because you really are going to get through it all today, but back here in realistic-land, according to when you *really are* going to do it … really.

Three factors govern the likelihood of actions taking place; firstly, the person who set the task or who is expecting the output. As Rachel, a very senior manager in the NHS, puts it, 'Even at my level, it's amazing how much keener I am to get on with something that's come down to me from the Chief Executive; it just seems to magically find its way to the top of the pile.' This kind of prioritization is not always in the best interests of the organization, as people at the top can be rather eccentric in their requests. But hey – that's their prerogative and we're not here to argue with it.

Secondly comes urgency; but it's a strange one, this, because one person's 'urgent' is another's *mañana*: judging what really is 'mission critical' is a matter of fine balance. There's an old debate raging as part of the time management agenda that says we're supposed to judge between urgent and important, but how exactly? The people who give us things to do often think that they are personally very important and it makes them feel more so if they tell us everything they need is urgent; logically it must be, otherwise we might start to question just how important they are, which would never do.

Making a call on what's important is a matter of context (maybe part of the context is who gave you the task – see above), but given any list of jobs, you're the best person to judge which comes before another.

Buggeration is the final contributory factor. We were going to find another word for it, but this seems to sum up the amount of hassle related to any task and it's a fair assumption that the greater the B-factor, the less you'll want to do it. Tasks that fit into this category are any that you are inclined to put off for any reason. It may be that they are unduly complex (spreadsheets!), or that your enthusiasm is dampened by not being able to see the point, or worse still, that they involve a series of actions that take you out of your comfort zone (cold-calling a list of new business prospects).

The worst thing about jobs with high buggeration is that they sap twice as much energy as they should do, because not only are they difficult when you get round to doing them, but, before then, they suck the enthusiasm from you as they nag away at the back of your mind, fretting over the fact that they're not done.

There's only one way of dealing with this and that is to programme it into your day map. Some would say get the B-tasks out of the way first thing, but we'd caution against that; it could ruin your day and what's more it might simply not be the best time. Take the telephone cold-calling example: start at 9 a.m. and most respondents will be busy easing themselves into the day, reducing your chances of success; much better to wait until later. Rather than let this become part of your natural procrastination, set an alarm on your watch, phone or wherever to go off at the time you have agreed with yourself to do the task and then, no matter what else you've embarked on, drop it, grit your teeth and tackle the monster.

Wayne, a successful sales executive says:

> 'We're supposed to like selling, but secretly I've always hated cold calling. Now I set a fixed time aside, find somewhere quiet and bash through it like a charging bull. I decided a good idea would be to set an end time to the task, so I had something to aim for and it's made me more efficient and less daunted; the spin-off (and I don't know why this has happened), is that my success rate has increased, too!'

Your action pile is only for the things that you'll do today, and it should be stacked in chronological order. Other priorities that don't need fulfilling today can form part of a future action pile, but don't let them clog up the current work in progress.

That's enough detox for one day; now you can get on with what you're paid for. But don't forget this next bit before you go home (on time).

RETROSPECTIVE

There are two quick things to do before finishing the day. The first is to write down one thing you found difficult today; it might be related to your detox, or it could just be a task, an interaction with a colleague or a difficult phone call – you choose. Make a note of it in your journal. Now also write down three things that you're pleased with; starting the day with a clear desk, feeling rehydrated and more energetic, defeating one of your 'buggeration' demons;

these are the kind of things you're aiming for. Look at the list for a few moments; take heart in your achievements.

JOURNAL

Record your feelings on the day as a whole at the foot of the relevant page of your journal by giving it a star rating; five is the most you can give.

HANG ON!

Last action of the day: take your paper clock off the computer and reflect on how well you managed to stick to the time.

PREP

You might be tidier, but how much cleaner are you? Even the best-managed offices with the most efficient cleaning service have their limitations, so part of tomorrow is going to be about spring-cleaning your workspace. This will include your computer, keyboard and mouse, desk surface and phone.

You can decide what the most suitable products to assemble are, but include a duster, some kind of polish and maybe a specialist screen cleaner (often found in the stationery cupboard), or a non-abrasive substitute. You might also consider making an early start tomorrow, so you can complete this task before everyone else arrives. Beyond your cleaning time, though, try to stick to your contracted hours. Once more, it's a great habit to get into.

FIFTEEN

DAY THREE

 ## CHANGE OF THE DAY

Today's change is all about what's happening in the world, what's in the news. There's a whole range of news consumption, from the junkie at one end, who watches endless hours on *News 24*, to the 'blissfully unaware', who thinks that there's not much to discover. In between these two, are modern-day 'Miss Marples' interested only in what's going on in their 'village'. Most Brits who visit America are astounded that much of the news coverage is parochial, focussing only on what happens in the state they're staying in. World news only seems to be covered if there's a 'local man' involved in it, giving some connection with the district.

Wherever you fit into this picture, take time out today to discover more. Actively seek out the news from four sources: national and local newspapers, radio, television and online.

Spare as much time for this task as you possibly can, but pledge to make it at least half an hour. This can be spread out over the entire day. Contrast the different ways the stories are handled, think about what each news item covers, try to see it from different angles and really think about what it means to you.

Of course it's true that there's not much coverage of good news; as they say in journalistic circles, 'If it bleeds, it leads', but that doesn't have to make the exercise all gloom and doom.

While consuming these current affairs, consider four aspects: the first of these is 'solution' – what could be done to remedy the state of affairs you find out about? Secondly, and related to this, try to focus on 'hope': what positive outcome might there be from conflict, or disaster, or man's propensity to inflict harm on fellow man?

'Change' is the third aspect to debate – what changes need to come about to make things better? Could you have any influence on that in the way you behave or the things you say?

And finally, as we said in the section on 'taking a walk' in Chapter 13 (p. 162), attempt to come to some realization of 'perspective': what is your part in local and world affairs? What impact does it have on you, or what impact do you have on it?

When you've thought about these four aspects, reflect on the impact of your discoveries in relation to your working life. This will have the effect of minimizing your own problems and strengthening your resolve to make more of what you do. The detox programme is designed to make life easier, and that should free up time for more important things. It doesn't mean you have to travel the globe sorting out its problems, but it could result in you taking a small, but positive action, which contributes to making life better for someone else.

So how was your shortened day yesterday? Did you feel more efficient because you knew there was a limited time to get things done by? A bit guilty about leaving before other people? A little worried that you didn't get everything finished?

The plain truth is that we never get everything done, either at work or in life, and imagine how awful it would be if we did! There wouldn't be any purpose to our existence any more. Start today by thinking about whether you're managing to get the *right* things done, most of the time; if and when the answer is 'yes', you're purging yourself of the toxins that bring most people down.

To celebrate the changes you're making, pour yourself a drink. A half-pint of cold tap-water will do for now; save the champagne for a while.

ACTION 1

Ten minutes is all you need for a quick spring-clean. Even if it could be scientifically proven that this doesn't make your equipment work better, it'll feel like it does. Start with your monitor screen, then, before you boot up your computer, give the keyboard and mouse the once over. Next, clean the phone mouthpiece and earpiece; don't even think about what it is that makes them look so mucky. Finally, a good spray of polish on the desktop and a quick wipe over with the added application of some elbow grease.

If you're thinking that all of this is a step too far, then consider the following; it isn't the outcome of this clean up which is of most importance, it's the *process*. By taking the time and trouble over your workstation that you might only reserve for your house or your car, you are staking a claim that this part of your life is important and worth taking a pride in. It's also clear to see that there is a positive result in terms of how it looks when you're finished, but you're not completing this action to impress your workmates, you're doing it to reduce your own toxins.

ACTION 2

Display some curiosity and interest.

We've been rather desk-focussed over the last few days, yet part of the ethos of detox is that you acquire the ability to see your working life in its entirety, each element of it interconnected with another. You will most likely have been able to see the connections between office and home life, too, so it figures that 'getting it right' at work will have some positive spin-off elsewhere.

This action is designed to get you off the production line and into the real world. The jobs we do in many modern businesses are built on the principle of a car manufacturing plant. It follows that if you can streamline each element of a process, by getting a specialist to complete it time after time, then productivity increases. When you stop to consider what it is that your company does, makes or services, it's easy to see how your part in it is just another cog in the wheel. In fact, it can soon become the case that we just do what we're told, and forget about the big plan. What's more, we stop wondering what our co-workers are involved in and how they're contributing to the whole.

Today you need to set 10 minutes aside to be curious. Find another process in the organization (it can be anything from the receptionist greeting people at the door, to the warehouse man signing goods out as they leave the premises) and talk to whoever does it. Even if you know how it all works together and understand in an intellectual way what everyone's job is, the learning behind this exercise is to discover what people *feel*.

And the point of all this? Often, in the workplace, we lack a sense of belonging. Firms today are no longer 'one big happy family' and we don't suggest for a minute that a short conversation with a work colleague is going to alter that forever, but what it should do is to give you an understanding of what happens to the mass of humanity around you each day. It might make you sympathetic towards others, or give you a greater sense of purpose in your own job. At the very least, you might make a new friend.

ACTION 3

You were beginning to think that we'd forgotten about the box at your feet, weren't you? Not a bit of it.

Detox works for lots of reasons, and each action you take is small and manageable, in a short timescale.

This is the case with this next action. It doesn't require any real physical effort, but a degree of emotional understanding is necessary. By now, all you should have left in your box are the personal effects you cleared from your desk. Typically these include the kind of items we mentioned earlier, like photographs and souvenirs, some reminder of your kids, maybe a picture they've drawn. These are lovely things, that speak volumes about you as a person and now you're either going to bin them or take them home.

This is a transcript of a conversation we had with Nick, a senior civil servant, in his office.

Interviewer: Who are the photos of [on your desk]?

Nick: Oh, that's me and my wife, not long after we met, and these are the kids, Jodie's fifth birthday party, and you can just about see Adam's face behind that huge piece of cake; he was only three then.

Interviewer: How old are they now?

Nick: Twelve and ten respectively.

Interviewer: And why do you keep these photographs here?

Nick: To remind me of them, of course.

Interviewer: (Provocatively) Is that because you never see them?

Nick: (Pause) Hmm, I'd never thought of it like that, but yeah, maybe.

It was possibly a bit harsh to put Nick on the spot like this, but there was a point to it. Very often we surround ourselves with evidence of our out-of-work life, to act as a touchstone when we're under stress. Nick said that when he was having a really bad day, he could look at the photos and it made him feel better, but when pushed on this, he found it hard to recall the last time he had done so. The pictures we put on our office walls become literally like wallpaper: we notice them (and whatever trinkets litter our desks) for a very short period of time, and then they're gone, consigned to our subconscious.

The only time they return to the fore is in a situation like the interview above, or when a newly appointed work colleague comes into your workspace and passes comment: 'Oh, is that your dog?' But they do this because they're meant to; you've prompted them into it by the display you've put up.

Very often the personalizing objects we bring into work are there for the benefit of others, rather than ourselves. They're a statement: 'Look! This is me, there's more than what you see – I'm a real person, with a real life, with relationships ... and a dog!'

Removing all of this doesn't diminish the person you are, but it does significantly de-clutter your workspace; the real importance, though, is that it de-clutters your mind.

If this sounds like one small action backed by a lot of justification then that's the truth of it, because we're often very closely wedded to the artefacts that personalize our work environment. We ran all of the concepts and principles in this book past our research group; the one they had the most difficulty with was depersonalizing their workspace.

So, if you have a heavy heart as you pack up your 'personals' in their removal box, you're not alone. If it helps, then think back to the interview with Nick: the part we haven't transcribed was when we asked him if, rather than gaze longingly at the photos of his loved ones as he toiled away at his desk, wouldn't he prefer to finish earlier each day and spend some real time with them instead? He found that hard to argue with.

RETROSPECTIVE

Get everything neat and tidy before you leave your desk: equipment put away, paperwork in a single pile and your computer shut down; then run your finger across the desktop to feel how

clean it is. That's how pure and uncluttered you should be starting to feel inside your head.

Have a final glass of tap-water and spend 30 seconds thinking
about the working life of the colleague you exercised your curiosity
on. Were they happy with work? Did they understand what was
going on in the rest of the company? Did your conversation
make a difference to their day? Paradoxically, it is normally the
things that we do for other people that make us feel better about
ourselves. A 10-minute chat doesn't turn you into a saint, but
maybe your showing an interest in someone else improved their
day just a little.

JOURNAL

Before you leave, take a couple of minutes to record your
thoughts and feelings in your journal. Try to capture how much
better it felt to be working in a clean environment, and if you
struggled with the depersonalizing process, record that, too.
Finally, give yourself an overall mark out of 10 for the day.

Now, tuck your box under your arm and go home.

PREP

Resolve is what you'll need tomorrow, rather than any physical
equipment, because you're going to detox the filing system. This is
the sort of job that achieves one of the highest buggeration factors
known to humankind, so instead of worrying about it, your prep
for this evening is to spend just a couple of minutes visualizing a
tidy and well-ordered filing system, both online and hard copy.

SIXTEEN

DAY FOUR

 CHANGE OF THE DAY

So far, our changes have all been about big important issues: going for a walk to reflect on our existence, changing the 'fuel' we use to improve our output, thinking seriously about world and local affairs so that we can consider our role in making things better.

As human beings we're tremendously complex and we can't always be expected to engage with the weightier issues that are part of our lives. In our research we came across some fascinating individuals, none more so than an eminent writer with a vast intellect; he could quote from Proust and Chaucer, lecture on the history and humanitarian issues of the Middle East conflict, but at the same time cited his favourite television programme as *Celebrity Big Brother* and best ever film as *The Karate Kid*!

All of these different aspects of our lives are part of what makes us human, so today is unashamedly about our propensity to gossip. Despite all the 'Men are from Mars, Women are from

Venus' theories, there seems to be very little evidence to suggest that one gender indulges more in gossip than the other. The way in which we do it might be different, but it's part of the human condition to be fascinated by lascivious trivia.

Some might choose pap magazines to find out the latest twists and turns in Peter and Jordan's relationship; others may be just as fascinated by the current rumour of takeover and boardroom shenanigans at a leading international conglomerate. It's all the same thing, really.

This change of the day is about difference, so whether or not your natural tendency is to dismiss some of the tittle-tattle that goes on, your task today is to find out what other people are gossiping about. It might mean buying a suitable magazine or just tapping into the chat at the water cooler, but remember: it's not what you hear that matters; it's how you interpret it.

Don't make the mistake of thinking that this seemingly trivial exercise isn't important, because gossip matters. It helps to shape opinion, it charts sociological change and it is often a welcome diversion from routine.

If you're still not convinced, think about the gossip that surrounded the huge Enron accounting scandal. This is a truly fascinating story in its own right but the repercussions have introduced a new term into the working methods of thousands of organizations. Now 'Corporate Social Responsibility' is big news in boardrooms across the land, with questions constantly being asked about the way we run our businesses.

You're over half way through your first week of detox, so start the day by reflecting on this fact and the part of the journey you've been on so far. Even before you get to work, imagine what your desk looks like now and then delve into your internal picture archive and think about what it was like on day one. Ask yourself the following three questions:

1   Do I have a better sense of order at work?

2   Am I more aware of where I keep things?

3   Has my efficiency increased?

The realization that a plan is coming together can make your heart race with excitement, so have a glass of tap-water to calm down.

So far, you've done some physical tidying up, had a go at altering the length of the working day, produced an action plan in the form of a day map and rendered your desk a work-only zone. With this degree of focus, your effectiveness should have already started to rise.

Today may prove to be the most exciting so far, as we set about sorting the wider working environment and filing both electronic and hard copies away, maybe forever.

ACTION 1

Stand at the door of your office, some way away from where your desk is, and complete an environmental scan.

What you're attempting to do is see where you fit into the broader picture of the workplace. By the end of the final day of this programme, your space should stand out from a mile away as a paragon of highly organized efficiency; an oasis of order in an otherwise chaotic clutter.

Wouldn't it be great if everyone around you was detoxing, too? Then you could make a real impact.

Occasionally, you hear stories of giant corporations attempting to enforce tidiness on their employees. We even know of a major international bank where senior managers were instructed to stay later than their employees and bin any paperwork that hadn't been put away for the night. If only they'd included our bank charges statements, too!

The first action of the day is to rethink the physical filing system. There's a spectrum of attitudes to filing. At one end is the ruthless de-clutterer who believes that they should action everything just once then bin the residue of evidence. Presumably they think that no one will ever ask them again about what they've done, or, if the occasion does arise, then somebody else in the company will have kept a copy. What's so annoying is that they're probably right; it's just that most of us can't bring ourselves to act that way.

At the other end of the scale is the 'never-throw-anything-away' merchant. We heard about a head of IT who issued an instruction that each employee could only have 10 megabytes of storage on the main server for their email, to stop it getting clogged up, but he had in excess of 3 gigabytes so that he could store every email he'd ever, ever received or sent. Please note that we may have exaggerated the actual amounts in the above story for dramatic effect.

Grasping the intellectual concept that huge archives of hard copy material are stored all over the country and will never be touched again is easy enough. The annoying thing about filing all this stuff away is that you're never sure which particular piece of paper you'll need again in the future, or how long it will be before you're asked for it.

Our attitude to filing is often the product of an imperfect memory; that's the kind that most of us have. We discovered this by forgetting something in the past: a birthday, an item we meant to buy at the supermarket, somebody's name. Having learned that we can't remember everything, we're naturally drawn to any perfect entity which can, and such a thing is supposedly a filing system. Because we know that it doesn't work if it's only 80% complete, we keep everything.

So, in the context of your detox, this is a powerful argument in support of filing systems, and you never thought we'd say that, did you?

The questions we really need to answer are where to keep it, for how long and in what way. If the system is already set up, does it work okay? If it does, then stick with it; if not, then what is your level of authority to change it?

Is there a difference between the 'whole-office' system and your personal files? Can you at least get your own house in order, even if you can't change the world? (It might be that, if this works out, people will see the efficiency of the way you work and start to copy you; it'll be like viral-filing, with the tidiness bug spreading each day!)

The secret with compiling a filing system to work by (if you have total control over it), is to subdivide it into categories that make sense to *you*, so you might do it by customer, or by date, or alphabetically; but whichever you choose, make it easy on yourself: adapt it to your personal memory strengths.

Archivist Gordon can't get away from his natural tendency to be meticulous; at home he even has all his movies filed on video in a strict order. Gordon's collection probably numbers around 200, but he only watches one every couple of months, so, if they weren't in order, would it matter that he may spend five minutes scanning the titles to find the one he wants?

Secondly, don't subdivide too much. Yes, it's always very impressive if someone can go straight to a piece of paper they filed three years ago, but as we've agreed, the vast majority of these things will never get touched again. It's enough to know approximately where something will be; the extra benefit derived from micro-cataloguing everything is outweighed by the time taken in doing it.

ACTION 2

Get decisive! It's not the most riveting job on the planet, filing, so the time taken up with it should be reduced to a minimum. Make some decisions. First, think about how *often* you're going to file things; the logical answer would be to suggest a little and often, so every time you encounter an item that needs to be stored, you do it there and then. The problem with this is that it cuts across the 'production line' theory of repetitive tasking; that's to say, when you're 'in the zone' for a particular job, you get better and quicker.

TARGET SETTING

Once a week, even once a month, is enough, but your action now is to decide *when*, then put it in your diary, otherwise filing will become top of the buggeration list. The benefit of logging when you are going to complete this kind of task is that you can stop it nagging away at you all the time. You're not constantly thinking, 'Oh, I must get round to doing that filing,' because you know exactly when that time is, which leaves you free to get on with other, more important things.

Next, decide *how long* you will keep things. This may be predicated on how much space there is. With filing of personal finances, utility bills etc., many people work on six months; beyond that it's not worth worrying about. A practical tip here is that every time you add the most recent document to the front of a file, you subtract the oldest one from the back and put it through the shredder.

Now consider the criteria you will use to judge whether to file or bin. It's easy with legally binding stuff – you know you have to keep that – but at the margins of importance are lots of other documents, so ask yourself if they are being replicated elsewhere and what is the worst that could happen if you couldn't find them again in future. These benchmarks should help you come to a decision. Try not to deliberate too long over each item, and before long you will have a mental scale of importance and will be able to come to much quicker conclusions.

The last stage in this process is the business of deciding where all this stuff is going to go; once more this is a logical process of prioritization. Customer files for people you have dealings with every couple of weeks can justifiably be kept in the nearest available cabinet, ready to be pulled whenever they ring. Less frequently used documents need to be as far away from your desk as is possible, without file retrieval being a major hassle. Most offices have basements or store rooms specifically for this purpose.

ACTION 3

You might be feeling a bit worn out by now, but just one more action and then you're done for the day. Whatever decisions you made about your physical files, do the same for the electronic ones.

If possible, archive some off onto a memory stick or disc. It's best to do this by date as the older the information is the less likely it'll be called for.

Keep big, chunky electronic folders in general categories, and only subdivide them when you have a logical reason for doing so. If, for example, you attend the same conference each year and compile data or take actions as a result of it, the main folder should be labelled 'conference' and the sub-folders should say what year – it's that easy.

If you're not particularly technically-minded, it can be a bit daunting when you start messing around with computer files: all those .exe suffixes and 'application data'; what on earth do you do with that? Just think of it as a collection of components that you don't recognize. If they were physical things, you'd put them in a box under your desk and stop stressing, so do the same with these. Just set up a folder of 'unknown things' then drag and drop the offending items in. If the IT repair man comes along in future, he'll be able to find them anyway, and if it's labelled properly, you'll remember what it's for, too.

When you go home tonight, look back over your shoulder at a clutter-free desk and an organized filing system, and give yourself the credit you deserve.

RETROSPECTIVE

There's lots of ground worth re-visiting during the detox, whether it's day-maps or drinking water, working hours or colleague interaction, but today has been a tough day. None of the decisions you've been asked to take is a major one, but there will have been plenty of them and this in itself can be draining. We've said before that the detox won't work if you try to do it all at once, so if there are days like today where you've concentrated all your efforts in one area, don't worry, because there's time to work on some of the other bits again as we go along. Instead, you should feel justifiably proud of achieving one of the major (and most boring) bits of detox.

JOURNAL

In your Daily Detox Journal, reflect on one thing you've learned from getting organized; is it that you're hoarding too much or filing things too infrequently? Write it down and say how you feel about it; then think about the day as a whole and pick an icon from these to represent an overall rating.

Now record whether or not the gossip you heard was of any use, and if the source of it can be trusted. You might like to find your own code for this, to avoid any future lawsuits!

PREP

So far we've dealt with lots of issues of ergonomics by getting our physical space in order. Tomorrow is going to be about work-flow, so on your way into the office, have a think about the things you're likely to be involved in and make a mental 'top three' list of priorities.

SEVENTEEN

DAY FIVE

 CHANGE OF THE DAY

For those of us who thought we invented popular music in the Sixties, there's a shock in store, not least because of the iPod generation that surrounds us now

Music is a massive part of the way people live today and the old generation gap that existed is breaking down all the time. Evidence of this is that, in amongst serious issues like the economy and education, politicians get asked questions about their attitude to the Arctic Monkeys.

The interesting thing about music is that it has always been an important part of our lives, being used as a source of pleasure, a way of expressing protest or a backdrop to a romance; we're often called upon to think about 'the soundtrack of our lives'.

Today's change is about 'switching stations' to find out what the 'soundtrack of other people's lives' sounds like. Tune into a different radio service, buy a CD that's outside your normal taste or download some tracks you'd never usually consider listening to.

To get any real, lasting effect, this is one change you might have to repeat for a few days, because it's easy to dismiss hip-hop as foul-mouthed rubbish or classical music as a high-brow cacophony of claptrap, but to do so is to 'diss' the opinions of a huge swath of society.

Instead, stick with it for a while and think about what it is that other people hear (and see) in their music. There are undiscovered pleasures awaiting you that can inspire, calm, shock or provoke thought. Try to find someone who habitually listens to this type of thing and ask them what appeals to them about it; you might get a new and unexpected perspective. *Vive la différence*, at least for a while, then you can put Wogan back on Radio Two.

The last day of the first week has arrived, so this marks the half-way point of your detox programme. Next week will focus on how to maintain what you've put in place, how to develop some new behaviours and the important business of fostering good relationships in the interpersonal parts of your working life.

Get the day off to a great start by taking pride in the fact that you'll come in to a clean and tidy desk. If 'residue' has built up over the week, put it where it belongs, either filed away or stored in its rightful place, awaiting use.

ACTION 1

This is the start of a work audit; an assessment of how much work is on your desk now, added to whatever else arrives during the day; from here you can discover objectively if you are making a net impact on your overall workload.

Take out a piece of paper and make a list of all the things you have to action; only include the 'knowns'. If you suspect that more responsibility is going to be placed on your shoulders further down the line, this doesn't count; only include what's current. List the jobs in a sensible format, not every single individual email that needs answering; instead you could group them into 'action', 'information', 'quick reply'.

Now, subdivide the list by date/time required. All the items that appear which need action today should be transferred to your itinerary, in the usual way; the others need to have timescales put beside them, so you have an idea what's coming up over the next few days, maybe the next week at most. Inevitably there will be longer term objectives you have to meet, but the further away the deadlines, the less focussed the action. You might have to complete a round of staff appraisals and know what the final deadline is, but until you have finished preparing for them and checked the diaries of the staff concerned, this is a job that will have to remain unscheduled: attempting to include it in this audit will only serve to cloud your thinking.

As we've said, the purpose of this exercise is to establish what flows across your desk, and whether you are making any impact on it. The reason that you're doing it in such a conscious fashion is to get away from vague feelings of 'always being busy' or 'snowed under'; you're attempting to see the wood for the trees!

ACTION 2

During the course of the working day, keep a log of everything you do that isn't already on your list; this will be needed for you to complete the next action. As tasks arrive on your desk, write down what they are, who they came from and a timescale in units, in the same way as you do for an itinerary. So, if it takes an hour, write a 6, if it's only 20 minutes, a 2 and so on.

Then go on to rate the task in terms of 'necessity'. If it's some urgent job which the Managing Director needs an answer on by this afternoon it gets a high score, but if it's just the start of another long-term initiative, downgrade your marking.

We can easily get swept up into thinking we simply have too much to cope with, but by assessing the genuine deadlines for each task, we're much more able to chart our work flow over an extended period, rather than thinking it all has to be done today.

During this process, you should also think about the implications of *not* doing some of these things. Remember the quotes from Andy McFarlane of IBM, who said that there's often only limited impact if some low priority things don't get done and that people are more sympathetic to you saying 'no' if you can present them with a valid, work-based reason.

ACTION 3

Set aside 10 minutes at the end of the day. Do this by deciding on a finish time and setting some kind of reminder, like the alarm function on your phone. If you don't, you'll suddenly find yourself ready to go home and won't have completed your audit.

Get both the lists that you made: the one from the start of the day and the ad hoc items list that you've made as each unforeseen piece of work has cropped up.

By putting the two lists side by side, you'll get a true picture of everything you've done, or need to do. The problem we often have is that we go home wondering how it is that we started off well-organized, with a clear focus on what was needed, yet go home feeling like we've achieved very little.

It doesn't matter how many of the items on your organized list you managed to get through, the important thing is the overall picture of how you spent your time. It might be that you set out with the best intentions, but got side-tracked along the way by the agendas of your work colleagues, or by actions that you couldn't have anticipated at the beginning of the day. Focus on how productive you have managed to be. Have you really done the things that matter?

Go through the list that emerged throughout the day, and categorize the items according to their necessity, or otherwise; so put a tick next to any tasks that are a real and important part of your job and a cross against anything that looks to you like 'fire fighting'. The crosses indicate the danger areas that you need to guard against tomorrow and in the broader

'A lot of jobs could be improved with a bit of creative thinking and I'm a firm believer in focusing on the old saying of "do the right things rather than do things right".' Lynn Rutter (Consultant, Organization Development, Oxfam)

future. What could you have done to avoid any of these things? Is it about better planning on your part? Do you need to 'fix' a particular area of your responsibility that seems to always throw up this kind of task? Or are the problems caused outside your immediate area of control? Are you being constantly asked to solve the problems caused by someone else's poor planning?

To make future days balance (i.e. have a more even spread of controllable items and fewer fires to fight), you need to raise your own awareness of the trouble spots and make it part of your planning to 'solve' the issues that cause disruption.

Set planning time aside in a future itinerary by marking whatever actions need to be taken in your diary; put 'by when' dates, so that you'll have some milestones to work towards. In the real world we can't always take account of other people's inefficiency, but coming to an understanding of how much impact this makes on any given day will help you to plan your time to take account of 'impending disasters' in the future.

RETROSPECTIVE

Consider your job in the context of your level of control. It's not likely that you get to choose what you do all the time; more often our own agenda is disrupted by the unexpected input of other people, so stop and think about how their job impacts on yours. How can you make these relationships work better, what do you need to COMMUNICATE to your colleagues, how and when will you do that?

JOURNAL

Reflect on how surprised you felt about the 'additional items' that altered your normal plan for the day. Ask how efficient your own planning is and if you may sometimes be guilty of needlessly disrupting someone else's work flow.

Finally, now that you've reached the half-way stage of your detox, stop and consider how far you've come up to now.

PREP

There is no prep tonight; you've come to the end of the first week and your reward is a work-free weekend. Switch off from the office and recharge your batteries with a bit of self-indulgence.

Were there any other surprises for you today? Perhaps you thought you had very little control and actually discovered that this isn't the case, or maybe you hadn't realised just how disorganized other people were. Record your thoughts in your journal, describe how satisfied you feel.

EIGHTEEN

DAY SIX

WEEK TWO

 CHANGE OF THE DAY

The point of 'change of the day' is to move us out of our comfort zone and give us the opportunity to 'see how the other half lives'. It doesn't, by necessity, mean that we have to make a permanent alteration to our values, wants or tastes.

Today's change is all about demographics; the categorization of communities and the changes that happen within them over time.

There has been plenty written about the difference between men and women, and an equal amount on the subject of the generation gap. Dissertations have been compiled on the merits and demerits of life as a toff or a chav. What is common to all is that most of us have found a level; one where we mostly mix with people like us, think like them and act accordingly.

This comfort zone is not in itself damaging in any way, but it stops us from understanding the lives and motivations of our fellow citizens.

The point of today is not to attempt to become like other people, but to understand the way they are. Rather than try to make a big leap into the thinking and motivation of a radically different person, we're only trying to get a flavour of how they live their lives and what shapes the way they see the world.

There are many ways of doing this, but one of the easiest is to scour the magazine racks in the newsagent's and pick up a few titles you'd never normally consider. Choose those aimed at the opposite gender and not within your normal age range. Scanning through a magazine aimed at teenage girls might well horrify you, especially in terms of its candid approach to sex and drugs and rock and roll, but it might give you some insight into what makes them tick and the influences and pressures that are part of their lives. Alternatively any 'quality' men's magazine will probably reveal just how confusing life is for them: are they supposed to still be 'new man sensitive', or is 'laddishness' back in fashion?

Change of the day has the overt benefit of sampling something new, but the real plus is that it gives us an opportunity to reflect on how different the rest of the world is from us, which brings us back to the issue of perspective. It's only when we can see the bigger picture that we have the opportunity to get our own lives into context.

The start of week two means a day of consolidation so that there's a firm foundation for the rest of the programme. New behaviours, like New Year's resolutions, are easy at first but much harder to sustain over time, so it's vital to embed all the good things from last week, before beginning a range of new challenges.

The widely accepted length of time it takes to change a single behaviour is four weeks, which is why advertisers encourage you to 'take the four-week challenge' with their product. Offering you your money back under these circumstances is virtually risk free because, for everyone who claims it, there will be dozens who successfully make the shift to their brand.

This detox halves the time to change behaviour; and you're able to do this for the simple reason that you spent considerable time and effort on preparing through the early chapters in this book. Once you've understood the rationale and pledged the commitment to these changes, it takes much less time to administer them successfully.

ACTION 1

The first thing to do today is work out how far you've come and then congratulate yourself on your progress. Start the day by writing down all the things you did differently last week, as a result of the detox programme. You will have already reflected on many of these things, but success is worth celebrating – it spurs you on to greater achievements. List any 'change of the day' which you have successfully completed: an increase in your hydration, clearer desk, better filing system or an understanding of what someone else in your organization does; anything that springs to mind as a positive step forward.

For each of the items listed, mark yourself out of 10 for how well you've done, so if you survey your desk and see that it's still as clear as when you de-cluttered it on day one, give yourself 10 points; if the filing has slipped behind a bit then reduce the tally for this task. This marking scheme will heighten your awareness of where you need to continue to concentrate your efforts.

From your list, now pick the top three things that have made an impact on your working life and write them down in order of priority. These are the areas you'll get most benefit from focussing on in the future, so it's worth recognizing just how valuable they are.

ACTION 2

It's likely that, whatever your intentions and actions, by now there will have been a bit of slippage, so you have 10 minutes to rectify the damage with a whirlwind spring clean. Before you launch into this like a dervish, take just a few seconds out, to reflect on what needs to be done and the order you'll tackle it in. Apply a bit of logic so that you don't end up undoing what you've already started. If new ideas, methods, systems or 'places to put things' occur along the way, note them down in your detox journal for future reference.

ACTION 3

Because our detox only takes a few minutes out of every day, there will inevitably be things left undone. Adjusting your mind-set to this can be difficult as you've set out on a process that is overtly designed to 'purify' your working space and existence.

The truth is that emails continue to arrive, objectives will carry on being set, dust will gather once again. Knowing this will stop you from going mad as, in your attempts to handle the 'toxins' of working life, you adopt a 'Forth Bridge' mentality: by the time you've finished one end, the other needs to be started again.

Revisiting what you've achieved on a daily basis is important. It helps you remember to restore your balance of tidiness, but also gives you the opportunity to achieve more. If you've already got into the habit of putting everything away at night, then you'll start with a fresh workspace every morning and if that's the case, you have a little spare time to get round to the jobs that never get done.

Make a list of these, like this:

◆ Clean computer keyboard

◆ Check all filing is completed

◆ Chuck away all 'redundant stationery' (pens that no longer work, pencil sharpeners that have gone blunt, etc.)

◆ Sort out the wire spaghetti under your desk

◆ Empty unused folders

◆ Ditch 'sleeping' projects (those where no action has occurred for weeks, or possibly even months)

◆ Slim down individual files (by archiving or disposing of the oldest paperwork in them)

◆ Consolidate all the Post-it note annotations onto one sheet and file or action them

◆ Return any 'borrowed' equipment or stationery: if you don't need it, put it back!

◆ Clean scanner or photocopier glass (so that copies come out like they should)

◆ Repair or replace anything that doesn't work (change light bulb in desk lamp, batteries in cordless mouse, etc.)

You will know best which things bug you the most, so prioritize your list in a way that suits you. There's nothing quite so frustrating as a stapler that always jams, or a pair of scissors that no longer work, so ditch them and get something that is fit for purpose. Although each of the actions may seem trivial in itself, every time you complete one you move nearer to your ultimate efficiency. The smell of a new car is universally appealing and, in the same way, sitting down to a keyboard that sparkles like new is much more desirable than the clogged-up version you might be more used to.

Computers are a big culprit when it comes to toxins. Often, they don't operate in the way they're supposed to, but rather than find a way around it ('I have to open email and then dial up the internet, otherwise the connection crashes …'), seek a permanent solution. If necessary, call on the services of an IT specialist, so that the bugs are fixed once and for all.

Often it is the collective uselessness of the things around us that can wear us out and reduce our effectiveness. It's also true to say that, on a good day, we just ignore the problem and battle on. But during the high pressure stress we experience when we have a deadline to meet, a photocopier that constantly jams can conspire to send us over the edge!

RETROSPECTIVE

It's not too early to have some new behaviours truly embedded. Think back over the day and consider the amount of consolidation that's taken place. A big part of this is tied up in the decision-making process that we go through a hundred times a day, and becoming firmer in this discipline is a big contributor to your overall success. Think about the level of resolve you're able to show and build on it, so that you can quickly assess the factors for consideration, weigh them in the context of your role as a whole and come to swift conclusions.

Today's given you the opportunity to think about and action some of the longer term energy-sappers; though the visible benefit will be a tidier environment, the best thing is the bit of 'mind-space' you've freed up: that part of your brain that kept on being nagged about what needed to be done.

JOURNAL

Log this de-cluttering of your mind in your journal and record what you intend to do with the thinking capacity you've released.

PREP

As tomorrow is aimed at the wider environment, and there's a focus on helping your colleagues, your prep tonight is to think about the things at work which cause 'universal annoyance'. Are the coffee mugs always left unwashed, is there too much paper wasted, do the doors on the filing cupboard stick because it's too full? Consider what it is that everyone else ignores and equip yourself to do something about it tomorrow (this may require you to take some bin bags in, or maybe a pair of pliers; it depends on the task).

NINETEEN

DAY SEVEN

 CHANGE OF THE DAY

This could well be the most difficult challenge you have yet faced in your daily changes, because today is about philanthropy. We don't assume that you are not already a well adjusted, caring member of society; it's just that all the current evidence points to a breakdown of communities and a lack of concern for our fellow man, so maybe we could all do a bit more.

We go through periods, sometimes for an extended length of time, when we feel that we're just about getting by, coping with everything that needs to be done, making ends meet, fighting to keep our heads above water. It's not surprising, under the circumstances, that we find little extra time to devote to 'worthy causes', but that's what today is about.

The difficulty with this task is that 'you can never find an old person when you need one'; if you do manage to track one down, volunteer to do a bit of shopping for them.

If you can plan an activity all the better – it doesn't have to be someone old; you could just offer a lift to a neighbour or look after their kids for an hour after school. Completing the task today would be preferable, but if that's not possible, a pledge of future good work will have to suffice.

After considering the options available, if you still haven't managed to come up with a suitable plan, you'll have to travel through the day with 'good intent', ready to step in and help whoever needs it, on an *ad hoc* basis. Most of us aren't usually in this frame of mind, so it's hard to see opportunities, but look out for them anyway and see if you can assist others.

You have to start from a point which says 'it's better to give than receive'. If you believe that, then you'll find very quickly that the good feeling you get from putting yourself out in favour of another will far outweigh any self-serving action you might otherwise have opted for.

When you're fully detoxed, there will be more time available for this kind of activity, and as well as increasing your overall happiness, you will be contributing, in a small way, to making the world a better place.

It's no coincidence that the actions in today's detox tie in with the change of the day.

Remind yourself before you set off for work today that detoxing your mind is as important as your desk, and think too about the role of rehydration in that. While you're doing so, you could idle away the time by drinking a glass of tap-water; by now this should be part of your routine.

When you arrive at work, scan your space, as you have done before, both as a check that things are still in order and a way of making your mental task list of things to do before you start. Clear away any clutter to where it now rightfully belongs and make out your itinerary.

ACTION 1

Include in it today, three actions that will help someone else achieve their objectives, according to your particular role. This might be anything from an offer of help with a colleague's tidy-up (maybe by now they've taken a leaf from your book and have started their own detox) through to departmental tasks, the sort that no one usually puts their hand up for. As a group, you might be responsible for customer contact or compiling a report, so your goal today is to take on more than your fair share of this.

If you feel like you already have enough to do, then the same probably applies to your colleagues and volunteering to do extra may seem like a burden. However, this achieves two things; firstly, it increases the likelihood that help will be reciprocated at some future date. Of course this isn't guaranteed, but if we're always looking for payback before we offer something ourselves, it's not really in the spirit of philanthropy.

The second achievement will be that you have displayed some 'discretionary behaviour'. These are the things we do over and above what's set out in our job description; it's what employers look for in their star performers.

ACTION 2

All places of work have areas which fall into nobody's remit in particular and it is often this which gives customers a basis for judging the organization. An example is to think about whose responsibility it is to keep the car park free from litter. You might have seen examples in the past where workers, even those in company uniform, will walk through a littered car park and ignore the detritus that surrounds them, never thinking to pick anything up; and this is all because they think it's 'not their job'.

You don't have to turn yourself into a one-person cleaning firm, but one empty crisp packet removed from the car park or one discarded tissue in a corridor, when multiplied by everyone in the firm taking responsibility, makes for a better working environment for all of you, and creates a massive shift in perception to customers.

If customers or other 'outsiders' see you doing this, it sends a clear signal about your pride in the company you work for, and might subsequently make them re-evaluate what a good organization it is.

Make three contributions to 'extra' tidiness; you won't have to look far to find litter, unwashed coffee cups or abandoned files.

ACTION 3

Think about the external relationships you have with suppliers, customers or partners. Which of these is most beneficial to you as an individual or the organization as a whole? Waiting for external contacts to get in touch often means that, by the time they do, it's because there's a problem. Knowledge of your role will give you the experience to judge what future problems might be, so make proactive contact with a third party and get on the front foot. It could be as simple as ordering fresh supplies of a commodity that you're always running short of, or speaking to a training provider to see what new courses they're offering. Anticipating these things will help to make sure that fewer fires need to be fought in future.

RETROSPECTIVE

Think about the effect of your actions today. How has your out-reach campaign made a difference to others? Making the choice to be less me-focussed, and giving other people a hand, has a dramatic impact on how you feel about yourself. All of this, added to a cleaner work environment, should leave you with the feeling that this has been a great day.

JOURNAL

As with previous days, feel free to record how the day went in your own words, but in addition, complete these three sentences:

1   Helping other people makes me feel …

2   My actions today had the effect of …

3   In future, I intend to …

PREP

Mostly we're brought up to believe that it's better to give than to receive, but the exception to this is in the field of communication. That's what we'll be looking at tomorrow, so think about the proportion of giving (speaking) you do, in comparison to receiving (listening). Take a piece of paper and draw your own version of this diagram, making the size of each organ relative to the amount of usage they get.

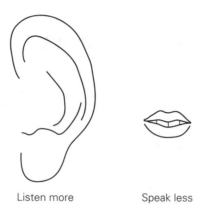

Listen more   Speak less

Look at it for a few minutes and try to imprint it on your memory, so that when you're in work tomorrow, it will act as a cue for the degree of listening you do versus talking.

TWENTY

DAY EIGHT

 CHANGE OF THE DAY

You needn't have the impression that the changes we suggest are some kind of campaign to return us to days gone by, when people took more responsibility for the world they lived in, but it's true that there is some degree of focus on making changes that benefit both us as individuals and the wider population.

It's easy to become frustrated or disillusioned about the behaviour of other members of society, but if we don't make some move towards positive action we're in no position to criticize. So today's change is about making a difference. It's to do with taking personal responsibility.

There are a million ways we can do this and you only have to find one. It could be as simple as having a clearout at home and taking all your unwanted items to a charity shop for the eventual benefit of a disadvantaged group. On the other hand, you might want to be more actively involved and seek out a volunteering opportunity, where you give some of your time and effort to a good cause. The choice is yours to make according to the issues you feel strongly about.

Alternatively you may get exercised by some wrong-doing close to home. It might be anti-social behaviour or noise pollution or fly-tipping. Whatever it is, it won't change unless we voice our disagreement. Challenging large gangs of youths on street corners or in shopping malls may not be your style and it certainly has its risks, but writing to your MP or lobbying the local council are ways of making your voice heard. Even a neighbourhood watch scheme contributes to the overall bonding of a community, so don't see these things as the preserve of some local busybody; get stuck in yourself.

If you're really pushed for ideas, scan the local papers and find out what the issues are around you, or do some research work on a global cause that upsets you, like famine or disaster recovery. A small, regular payment to a charity of your choice can make a big difference, especially when added to the contributions of others, but just as good can be the donation of your 'services' to help decorate an old person's home, or do their shopping once in a while.

Often it's not just what you're seen to be doing which is of benefit. The real bonus, as with some of our other changes, is the way it makes you *feel*.

When things go wrong in the workplace and it looks like there may be no one else to blame, we can always turn to a tried and tested scapegoat: 'communication'. Wars have probably been started and countless relationships ended, all because of a 'breakdown in communication'. Someone once said that 'patriotism is the last refuge of scoundrels'; they were probably paraphrasing and meant 'communication breakdown' instead.

In the workplace, too, communication is at the root of all ills. It's always a case that 'them up there never let us know what's going on'; and when we eventually become one of 'them up there', it seems we're no better.

The massive changes in technology that have come about over the last 20 years have also made this situation worse. If once there were people who couldn't quite read the smoke signals, this has now been made worse by faxes, emails, text messages, blogs, voicemail, teleconferences and more. The proliferation of choice has only added to the confusion.

But just as a bad workman always blames his tools, it's true that the technology and the channels of communication aren't at fault. it's the operator who has to bear the brunt of the blame. A lack of education about good email practice might, for example, go some way to explain this modern workplace malaise, but, and let's be honest about this, there is just as much *wilful* misuse of the tools as accidental.

It seems like none of us are any good at handling conflict, so why not avoid it and discipline staff by sending them an email? (Some have gone further and actually sacked staff by text message.) Alternatively, when you want to dump a load of your work on somebody else, it's much easier to do it from behind the safety of your screen than to physically plonk the folders on their desk.

Although this is prevalent, it's nothing new; people have always blamed the messenger, the message or the mode of delivery. The conversation overleaf was overheard in the offices of a large multinational company in the Seventies.

Bob: Can you get this sent off to Ceylon?

John: Yes, sure, errm it's not called Ceylon any more, though.

Bob: Isn't it?

John: No Bob, it's Sri Lanka now.

Bob: Well, no one sent me the memo!

Liberate your ostrich head from the sand today, and make a promise to start using the tools of communication properly.

ACTION 1

If you've still got a trillion emails languishing on your desktop (and you shouldn't have by now – see *Day Four, Action 3*), it's time to sort them out. Highlight everything that's over six months old and, if you're feeling brave, press the shift and delete keys (this removes them from your machine, rather than just clogging up your 'deleted' box). For the faint of heart, there's a safer alternative: you could just choose to back up the backlog, but really, you're not going to need any of them again, so why not just get rid?

Cutting back on the number of emails you have to answer is trickier, but start to think of email like flirting: the more you encourage the other party (by replying to them), the more they will 'come on' to you. Yes, you will still need to answer 'mission critical' emails from the boss, but in reality, lots of the stuff that arrives could be defined merely as 'nice to have': just scan them, then bin them.

Email has become like a modern day version of the game-show 'clapometer'. It's not the *volume* of sound it makes that is important, but the *frequency* with which it 'chimes'; this becomes an indicator of how popular we are and every time it goes off, just like a ringing telephone, we feel compelled to find out who is trying to contact us. These constant interruptions to the focus you're trying to apply to your work make it really difficult to concentrate and, as a consequence, they damage your efficiency.

Turn the sound off on your computer, so that you can't hear the alert of incoming email; then minimize the programme so that you have no visual cue to signal the arrival of new mail. This is so you can be the master (or mistress) of the inbox, not the other way round. In your itinerary, get into the habit of scheduling email time in chunks that are no longer than 20 minutes then focus on what you have to get through. Put your head down and power your way through it; you'll be amazed how much you can accomplish.

ACTION 2

When Alexander Graham Bell invented the telephone, he thought he had developed a device whereby two people in different locations could converse. What he didn't realize was that the by-product of his efforts was to also produce an instrument with almost magical powers, which, once ringing could not – under any circumstances – be ignored.

People get out of the bath to rush to their phones (but they always stop ringing at the critical moment); with mobiles, they answer while driving. There may be more extreme cases – during childbirth for example, or while balancing on a high wire!

This practice has become so much a part of our normal jobs that we can't just leave a phone to ring; it does need answering. Accept this fact and manage your phone calls.

Again, your itinerary will provide a solution to outbound calls: plan them when it suits you or, if you're in a service role, when it suits the customer. Bundle your outbound calls into chunks of the day (20 minutes is a good time-frame again), then just get on with it.

With inbound calls, don't waffle, cut to the chase; without being rude, ascertain quickly what the point of the call is (N.B. doing this will make you realize that many of the calls you receive have no point at all, or the communication could have been handled more efficiently by another means, but this is the caller's problem, not yours). Summarize back the actions that need to be taken (if there are any), and set a time-frame you'll respond by. This is important in putting you back in control.

The telephone allows you to multi-task in a low level way. If you devote 80% of your concentration to the caller (and, depending on who it is, you can sometimes reduce this!), then use the remaining 20% to do another useful task, like tidying your desk. A headset or hands-free connection can be a real asset here, as it allows the freedom to email while you talk!

ACTION 3

Personal communication, face-to-face, is the most powerful of all – that's why it's reserved for important business dealings (sales pitches and presentations, etc.). The last thing you should do with such a valuable commodity is trivialize it with pointless meetings.

You don't always get the choice, but in any meetings you have today, try to focus. Ask yourself, 'What am I doing here? How can I contribute more? What is the point of this meeting?'

If you're struggling to understand the purpose of a meeting, ask yourself these three questions afterwards:

◆ 'What did I learn?' (Is there information you took away with you, which you didn't know at the start?)

◆ 'What did I teach?' (Did you convey anything to the other meeting participants they didn't know or couldn't have found out somewhere else?)

◆ 'What did we decide?' (This is the tough one, because in the real world, many meetings don't come to firm conclusions.)

Also try to be aware that actions which people agree to undertake should have a 'by when' date against them, or, like many things, they can remain not done indefinitely.

As we said at the start of this action, face-to-face contact can be an incredibly effective way of communicating, probably the best there is, so reserve it for the things that matter.

RETROSPECTIVE

Before you leave work today, make a rough mental calculation of the percentage of time usually wasted by the domination of other people's communication. Consider the swaths of useless email they send you, the completely pointless phone calls you receive and the unfocussed meetings you're called to.

Detoxing the communication on your desk, and in other parts of the office, will put you back in control of these time-stealers, so constantly ask yourself in the coming days, 'Do I need this? Is it just a "nice-to-have"? How does it help me to do my job or assist someone else in theirs?'

If you're being totally honest and frank, you will also face up to the fact that you, too, have burdened other people with the kind of toxic communication we've covered here. So think about the impact on your co-workers' inboxes, and the benefits to their time management, that a change of heart, direction and focus on your behalf will make.

Now, have a glass of water and go home.

JOURNAL

List the three most useless sources of communication you regularly encounter. This might include people who habitually steal your time with email, or a meeting you're forced to attend. By doing this, you will highlight the 'villains'. Promise yourself that you'll try and marginalize them in future.

Now, write down your most useful source of communication and record how you feel about today's actions.

PREP

As the end of your detox approaches, you'll have a chance tomorrow to build on what you've done and get round to one of the longer-term jobs you've been putting off for ages. Save yourself some thinking time in the morning by deciding now which of the tasks you're going to assault.

TWENTY-ONE

DAY NINE

 ## CHANGE OF THE DAY

Keeping some kind of balance between work and leisure is an ongoing battle, and what it sometimes results in is us being too tired to be bothered with new diversions. For that reason, today's change is designed to take you out of your normal sphere of 'entertainment' and get you to try something new.

At the very lowest level, this might mean switching channels as you veg out in front of the TV after another exhausting day at work, but you can do better than that, can't you?

Maybe your town or city doesn't have anything exciting to offer this evening, but you can still turn your intent into action by booking something and putting it in your diary. Live entertainment comes in many forms; maybe there's a local jazz or folk festival coming up, or check out the listings at the local theatre and don't be bound by what you would normally see: try Chekhov or Shakespeare, have a bash at a musical or spend some time at a stand-up comedy gig; there's plenty to choose from.

Alternatively, a visit to a museum or art gallery can be inspiring and uplifting; just have a go at an entertainment that's passed you by. If all else fails, visit the library or a bookshop and give yourself sufficient time to have a good look at what's on offer; try to choose an author you haven't read before, or pick an entirely different genre to freshen up your perspective.

Even if you don't like it, you'll be able to express an *informed* opinion about it in future, rather than letting your dislike appear as bigotry.

With only a couple of days to go before your detox is complete, you might be starting to panic about getting it finished. Whatever your personal gap is, use the day to narrow it down, because each percentage point achieved is another small step towards reaching your target.

Today is going to be about building on what you've achieved in your detox so far. Some of this will mean going back over ground you've already covered, but there's also an opportunity to practise some good habits you've begun to form and there's advice on how to use the commonly found tools of the office with more efficiency.

ACTION 1

Perform your scan of the workspace when you first arrive and check that the desk is clear, the filing is under control and your environment is tidy.

Spend 10 minutes having a quick look through the desk drawers to see if there's anything else that's surplus to immediate requirements and then bin it, give it away or return it to where it came from.

Switch on your computer and check that the desktop isn't cluttered with icons that you don't understand or never use. If there are any, consign them to the folder you created earlier.

Reflect on how much more efficient your system is, then move on to the next action.

ACTION 2

Create an itinerary that includes all the tasks you know about specifically, then add in some contingency time based on your new knowledge of a typical workflow. Choose one task that would normally be on your 'long term' list, maybe organizing or creating some system, updating records, or contacting customers. Don't be tempted to pick more than one, because although it's good to have a target that stretches you, underachieving on several fronts can just leave you more dissatisfied than when you started.

These longer-term objectives normally find their level at the bottom of the pile and remain there for long periods, because they're not vital to our everyday lives, but the fact that they remain undone is something that silently nags at us and uses up a percentage point or two of energy, every single day.

Make a point of building in 20 minutes (2 units), of 'free thinking' time on your itinerary and keep it to one of the most alert parts of the day, according to what you now know about your personal energy cycle.

Use the time to focus on one long-term objective that usually has a negative impact on your efficiency within the business and note down, in your journal, all the possible solutions. After that, think about the barriers to each potential course of action and choose the answer that you feel is most likely to succeed.

In tandem with this, consider the extra commitment (in terms of people, resources, or attitude) that might be required, and set a date in your diary for when you'll tackle the first 'milestone'.

Now, map out your important work for today and get started on it, but also set a time at which you're going to start on your long-term priority, and stick to it. The final part of your day mapping is to decide on a finish time and set an alarm for 10 minutes prior to it, just so you have time for a quick tidy-up before you leave. Try to make sure you work a 'standard' day and get everything completed within your contracted hours.

ACTION 3

The final part of today's programme is concerned with the way you communicate. Build on the heightened awareness you gained yesterday, with particular regard to email, telephone and face-to-face communication. Now set yourself a time limit for each mode of contact and think about when in the day you are going to action each. Use your day map to plot these blocks of activity.

If this is partly driven by other people's actions, as in the example of meetings, you will need to work around it, but don't lose the will to change your behaviour when you attend; think about the benefits of being there and set your objectives accordingly.

Chunk email and outbound telephone contact into 20-minute time slots and save 30 seconds at the end of each period to reflect on how much you achieved against what you thought you'd do.

Just as an athlete aims to beat their best time when they train or compete, you can set the standard for your own 'personal best', getting through more on each occasion that you take on this task.

Make a diary note of all the other non-urgent, but niggling, tasks and log when, in the next month, you're going to tackle them.

RETROSPECTIVE

When you look back on the day, pay particular attention to the long-term problem you started to solve. Knowing that this task is now underway should make you feel better about your progress and spur you on to repeat the exercise in future.

JOURNAL

Catalogue any specific difficulty you encountered in today's detox; also record the success you had in starting to deal with one of your long-overdue tasks. Write down three things you've learned from the detox process so far and give a reason why they have helped you.

PREP

There's no formal prep for tomorrow as the day is going to focus on looking back at what you've done so far, reminding you of the key points of the detox and celebrating your success.

TWENTY-TWO

DAY TEN

CHANGE OF THE DAY

No matter how many machines, how much technology or how big an infrastructure contribute to our working lives, by far the most important element is 'people' and our relationship to them.

Whether we're talking about colleagues, customers or stake-holders, business only works (or sometimes fails to) because of the people involved in it.

It is the state of these relationships that can make us happy or miserable, and this is heightened tenfold with the people in our lives who are unconnected to work. What happens to many of us is that we get so tied up in our working lives that we don't have enough time to devote to nurturing, developing and sustaining the relationships that would be key to our happiness. So today's change is about reconnecting with someone important.

You could simply cook a meal or buy a gift for a spouse; you might ring your mother to see how she is; or make some meaningful contact with someone from your Christmas card list, who you promise to get round to seeing soon, but never do!

If you're feeling really ambitious, we recommend you write a letter. Although this form of communication seems to have fallen into decline with the advent of email, etc., there simply is no better way of showing that you care. It has the added benefit of making both you and the recipient feel good.

Many of our dissatisfactions are caused by relationships that aren't working properly and, in most cases, this is not due to a lack of *ability* to engage with other people, but a lack of time.

Our happiest childhood memories are seldom to do with receiving a new toy; they're almost always connected to an *occasion,* when we spent time with the people closest to us.

Replicating this means making time to show that you care about someone and that might turn out to be the most significant 'change of the day' of the whole programme.

You've reached the last day of your detox and you should be feeling rightly proud of yourself. It would be no surprise if you've had times when you've asked, 'Why am I doing this?' But the answer is not just simply that you wanted to have a tidy desk, because our workspace is only a representation of who we are and what we stand for.

Detoxing your desk is the first step to de-cluttering your life and mind, but even this much grander aspiration does not in itself make you a better person. It is only a method, a tool that gives you the opportunity to make more choices about what you do next.

One final push is needed to get you over the finishing line.

ACTION 1

It's time to assess just how far you've come and to make some promises about what will happen next. The first thing to do is to complete a thorough appraisal of your workspace. Refer back to the audit you made, either in terms of the photos you took, the drawings you did or the list you filled out, which charted your starting position. Compare this to the way things are now. Is your desk uncluttered, have you got the filing under control, does everything have a place and is it in it?

The physical surroundings are a really important part of making an objective judgement of how far you've come, but there's more.

Detox is meant to make you feel better, so look at the following sliding scale, which has a pointer set to the middle. In comparison to how you might have felt a fortnight ago, how far can you move the pointer up the scale? Study each of the areas listed below and mentally move the indicator to the level you think you're at. What's your score now? Would it have been lower a fortnight ago? If so, how much higher is it now?

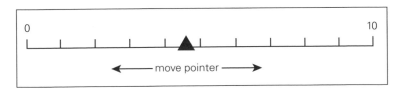

- ◆ Level of tidiness

- ◆ How well organized do I feel?

◆   How efficient do I feel?

◆   How satisfied am I with the outcome?

◆   How much more liberated do I feel?

◆   How much more in control do I feel?

◆   How much happier am I?

◆   To what degree is my desk detoxed?

◆   How much is my mind de-cluttered?

ACTION 2

Although the programme is coming to a close, you are not at the end of the process. Detox is only a means and method of starting to work, think and live differently; for it to be truly effective, you have to sustain the behaviours you've been using. Here is a reminder of the key elements of the detox; the things you'll have to continue to focus on in future. Read the list a few times, then see how many actions you can remember. Make a diary note to come back to this in a week and try again.

◆   Keep your desktop clear. Use it for work in progress, not pending

◆   Everything has a place. Make sure it stays there until you need it, then you'll know where it is

- Remember to regularly rehydrate yourself – it's essential for good concentration

- Don't let others steal your time: stay in control and keep focussed

- Helping other people benefits you both

- Try new things. Plan them, then do them!

- Make time to think

- Eke out your face to face communication, it's a valuable tool

- Keep a folder for filing and make diary entries to do it regularly

- Get on with the daunting jobs; they take less energy to do than you think

- Depersonalizing your workspace helps you to focus

- Keep the desktop clear by tidying up regularly

- Don't try to multi-task; do one thing well, then the next

ACTION 3

In many senses your detox is now complete. Congratulations!

To celebrate, you can plan your own one-person party. (Invite others if it makes you feel good!) Your reward for getting this far is a matter of personal choice, but don't let the moment go unrecognized. Take the time to explain to a colleague or friend the process you've gone through; tell them why and say what improvements you've made. Articulating your progress in this way helps to make you conscious of them in your own mind and to consolidate for the future.

RETROSPECTIVE

When you get home tonight, think about all the good things you've done during your 10-day detox. Reflect on the journey you've completed and how it's made you feel.

Now, go and pour yourself a glass of water, or, if you prefer, something stronger.

JOURNAL

Record your feelings about today's work and map out the significant changes you've made over the whole programme. Include the thoughts, feelings and actions that have made a difference. Don't be afraid to log some of the negatives, like the barriers you encountered, but try to counter-balance this by thinking of solutions.

Complete the following sentence.

'The detox programme has made me feel ...'

TWENTY-THREE

POST DETOX

YOUR FUTURE

To stay detoxed, there are some actions you'll need to revisit from time to time; the frequency of these visits is up to you. Make diary entries for weekly, monthly and quarterly updates; add in some 'changes of the day' of your own and keep up the momentum of your improvements so far.

There have been a number of exercises to complete during the course of this programme, aimed at auditing or logging your position, and you will remember that we made reference to the fact that this is so you can see how far you have journeyed.

In order to do that, you need to revisit some activities.

On your final detox day, you were asked to look back on the state of your desk at the start. If you have digital photographs, get them out and compare them to how things are now; if you've been really good and kept your workspace clear, take some more photos and then pick one from each batch to show a 'before' and 'after' scenario.

Attach these to the frame of your computer monitor or some-where else that's in direct line of sight and keep them there for a week, before binning them. They will serve as a physical reminder of your detox. (If you keep them longer, they'll stop being noticed and will start to become clutter!)

Next, monitor how well you can complete an input and out-put exercise. Refer back to the first time you did it and think about how accurate it turned out to be: is your level of awareness heightened now? Can you be more specific about where work comes from and where it goes to? Are you better at processing what comes onto your desk?

Finally, in conjunction with this exercise, draw up a new time cake and map the broad areas of activity as you did before. What level of control do you now have? Are there strategies you em-ploy to stop other people stealing your time? Have you learned how to negotiate harder for what's on your agenda, instead of being driven by theirs?

Armed with this efficiency audit, assess its worth in the context of your life as a whole by revisiting the areas of **control**, **balance**, **relationships** and **happiness** (page 97) and scoring these, once more out of 10.

Over the coming weeks, don't get downhearted if some of the disciplines of the detox start to slip and your level of control over work versus life suffers as a consequence. By completing the programme, you have proved to yourself that you're able to exercise greater levels of self-discipline, work in a more efficient way and stop allowing others to set your agenda. You can take back this control again.

Over the coming days, take a few moments each morning to look at your journal, partly to remind yourself of the new behaviours you committed to and also to motivate you to carry on with the procedures you've put in place for yourself.

Although the changes we've made have been small ones, by building up each day it's amazing how much more efficient we can become. We recognize that it can also be quite draining, simply because all changes, even minor ones, result in a degree of anxiety at first, so don't be surprised if you feel worn out!

Take a break and, for a few days, just try and make sure that you don't slip back to where you were before. After that, you might like to try a few new detox tips, each of which will have just as big an impact on your life.

Mark a date in your diary, logging when you'll come back to this chapter, then choose the extra detox that you feel most comfortable with.

ADVOCACY

One of the really tough things about this programme is that, for most people, they'll be ploughing a lonely furrow – one which might even threaten the security of their work colleagues because, inevitably, as you become more efficient, there is the risk that they will look less so, in comparison. But the spirit of detox is not to make you better so that you can gain advantage over your peers. It's focussed solely on making your working life more effective, for all the benefits we've mentioned, like job satisfaction, better time management and a restoration of some kind of sensible balance between your work and home life.

If it's worked for you in the way it has for others, you might like to suggest (tactfully) to one of your colleagues that they try it for themselves. It might be that they actually volunteer! When you consider the difference that the programme has made to your working life, think about how much better that could be in an entire organization that had detoxed. Working in a company whose team members are considerate to each other, where the use of time is at maximum efficiency and the culture supports people delivering their output mainly within their contracted hours would be a major step forward for most of us in our working lives.

COACHING

You will have learned throughout the process of detox what went well and what you struggled with (if you need to jog your memory, the daily journal you completed will help in this), so you're the person in the best position to say, 'If I did this over again, these are the things I'd watch out for.' You now have the benefit of being able to pass the process, and the experience of undergoing it, on to somebody else.

Rather than look for shortcuts or make alterations to the programme, think instead about the elements where you under-anticipated the level of difficulty or the great successes you had; for example, how easy you now find it to keep up to date, or how much more efficient your communication has become. These are the things that you can pass on, which will make the process easier for other people.

Volunteer to act as a detox coach, so that the next user has the advantage of being able to complete their daily journal, and also to discuss with you the good things they've done and the difficulties they face. This kind of 'live' coaching is a fantastic way of motivating people and it's guaranteed that *you'll* learn and grow during the process.

Try to remember that coaching is about helping other people to find their own solutions, so don't be tempted to 'tell them the answer'; instead, listen intently and ask what alternatives they can think of to solve their own problem.

DETOX YOUR HOUSE

How you live is up to you. If your house is messy, that's fine, as long as you're happy with it. However, the chances are, after you've detoxed your working life, you'll be less satisfied with living in a space that is cluttered and inefficient. The mess that surrounds you will start to get on your nerves and this will be made worse on the occasions when you're rushing out of the house and can't find your car keys or your glasses.

Having a 'place for everything' is as much of a help at home as in the office, so make conscious decisions about where things should 'live'. Make a point of always leaving your specs in the same place, find a home for the car keys and put them there every time you come home. It'll make life a lot easier.

Just as at work, lots of the things we surround ourselves with are a product of *heritage* or *habit*; they've always been there and we've stopped noticing them. When it comes to having a clear-out, there are only three categories to consider: function, aesthetics and sentiment. Everything in your home should be there for one of these reasons; it either does something (kettles, televisions, vacuum cleaners, etc.), it looks good (soft furnishings, ornaments, pictures, etc.) or you have some emotional attachment to it (gifts you've been given, things your children made for you, etc.). Beyond this, every other item is classified as clutter and needs to be disposed off.

Do this thoughtfully. Rather than take it all to landfill, give things away, to friends, neighbours or a charity shop. Once it's all gone, you'll be amazed at how much more space you have, so avoid cluttering up again in future by remembering the three categories we've listed: only allow items to cross the threshold of your home if they fit into one or more of them.

DETOX YOUR TIME-KEEPING

Take the fundamental principles of this programme and apply them to your punctuality. Many of us mean to be on time for things, but never seem to achieve it. *Intent is the antithesis of action*, so analyse your weak spots, set some daily objectives, keep a reflective journal and see how much you can achieve in the next 10 days.

When you have important deadlines to meet or a rendezvous at a particular hour, time backwards from it and make a realistic assessment of what you can get through between now and then. Factor in some room for additional interruptions, add 10% to the prep time of the critical meeting, leave early and, if you get there ahead of schedule, use the spare time to revisit your prep, so that you look even more efficient once the meeting starts

The experience of detoxing your desk will help greatly in making these assessments and, by recording the results, you'll see how much you've achieved and how much more work and effort you need to put in to ensure your future punctuality.

DETOX YOUR FINANCES

Get organized by mapping out where your money goes. The huge number of transactions we complete, the increase in direct debits from our account and the universal popularity of credit cards means that lots of our expenditure goes unnoticed. Heighten your awareness by listing your regular items, then taking them away from your monthly income.

Although this can come as a shock, it's also your financial reality and to make your spending even more conscious, convert the balance (i.e. the amount you have left to spend) into cash and ditch the credit cards for three months. If you're paid monthly, divide the cash into four envelopes, one for each week. Don't allow yourself to open an envelope until that week has begun. It's a great way of waking up to where your main expenses lie.

These are just a few suggestions of how to take the principles of detox into other areas of your life. What else you do with it is up to you, but, in order to help, here is a collection of tips from the 'Pertinent Post-its' and main text of the book.

◆ Avoid denial by comparison

◆ Own up to what needs detoxing

◆ Make a plan, set a date

◆   Detox over 10 days; change something every day

◆   Apply the process of wake up!/realize/decide/go! in order
to prepare

◆   Log the 'before' picture in as graphic a way as you can think
of

◆   Remember the importance of reflection; keep a daily detox
journal

◆   Make your actions short and sharp; build on new ones each
day

SOME FINAL THOUGHTS

We started by saying that the book shops are awash with self-help
titles that claim they will make you a better person. In writing
this book, we've tried really hard to avoid any such extravagant
claims, simply because we don't think that you need to change
in that way. Mostly we feel that the differences they tell you that
you're supposed to make to yourself are far removed from where
you are now; all of that 'anyone can become President' stuff we
talked about at the start just isn't a reality.

It's not that we advocate setting your aspirations too low, but always 'shooting for the stars' can be demoralizing because aiming
too high will often result in you falling short of your goal, and all
that serves to do is to fuel feelings of being an underachiever.

Detox your Desk is about clearing the clutter from your workspace,
but it's also designed to free up your thinking about all of your

life. We believe that by keeping it steeped in reality, by emphasizing that, for most of us, our lives are populated only by low-level dissatisfaction and that by changing something small every day and re-educating ourselves into tiny revisions of habit, we can make a significant difference in the things that really matter to *us* – without feeling guilty about not running for President.

Change is great, it's exciting, but it's also scary and the tough truth is that it's really hard to maintain over time. Again, you shouldn't feel guilty if you look back in a year and find that you've slipped into some of your old ways; it's human nature. However, you have the advantage of being able to run through the programme again: just re-read the daily detox actions, or remind yourself, through a dip into your Daily Detox Journal, what you set out to achieve, how you did it and the way it made you feel … Maybe that, more than anything, will spur you on to greater heights.

Working life has never been more difficult. The demands placed on us are a greater burden than ever before, but work is only a part of our lives and we owe it to ourselves to keep it in context. You will have heard the well known saying that 'no one on their death bed ever said they wished they'd spent more time at work', which, as well as its more obvious meaning, hints at work being a bad thing, something we dislike doing.

If detoxing your desk allows you a bit more time *out of work* and gives you the opportunity to *enjoy it more when you're there,* then the process has all been worth it.

Thanks for giving it a try.

Glass of water anyone?

INDEX